Sally Patton brings an enlightened perspective on how to parent from a balanced place of love, and beautifully articulates the idea of changing one's Mind about their children rather that trying to fix them. The importance of moving past the labeling of our children and experiencing the essence of the Spirit is not ignored in this book. Don't Fix Me I'm not Broken *is a God-send to anyone who wishes to join with their children rather than separate, love rather than fear, and accept their Divinity rather than deny their perfection.*
Gary Renard, Best-Selling Author *Disappearance of the Universe* and **Cindy Lora-Renard** MA Spiritual Psychology.

Don't Fix Me, I'm Not Broken is an extraordinarily helpful book. It is unique in its approach and aim. It asks us to open ourselves to the deeper meaning behind our children's seeming condition. It invites us to be willing to renounce our human story about this condition and to ask the Divine to reveal the lessons of love that await our welcome. "I see you, not the behavior, not the condition or the label; I see the truth of you."
Nouk Sanchez and **Tomas Viera**, authors of *Take Me to Truth; Undoing the Ego* From the Foreward to *Don't Fix Me, I'm Not Broken*

Sally Patton asks us to look past the diagnostic labels we give to children, and see the radiant spark of the divine. Her book serves as a soothing balm to comfort parents who feel overwhelmed by the challenges of raising an atypical child. I recommend it highly!
Thomas Armstrong, Ph.D., author of *Nuerodiversity: Discovering the Extraordinary Gifts of Autism, ADHD, Dyslexia, and Other Brain Differences, The Myth of the ADD Child* and *7 Kinds of Smart*

An insightful book that helps parents to come from love rather than fear when facing a child's disability, disorder or disease. Sally Patton proposes a wonderful perspective; our unhappiness does not solve our children's problems, it is our clarity and comfort that has the most beneficial impact.

Barry Neil Kauman, Best Selling Author: *Happiness is a Choice* Co-Founder of The Option Institute and Autism Treatment Center of America

Sally Patton's Don't Fix Me, I'm Not Broken *builds upon the tenets from* A Course in Miracles *to inspire parents toward a new standard of understanding: to perceive their relationships with sons and daughters through a spiritual prism — one that is invaluable for its wisdom about acceptance and its lessons in unconditional love.*

William Stillman, author of *Autism and the God Connection* and *The Soul of Autism*

Don't Fix Me, I'm not Broken *is a book that goes right to the center of the heart. This book helps cultivate an awareness of unconditional love and acceptance — a power that can heal the world.*

Jared Rosen, Founder of Dreamsculpt Media Co-Author of *The Flip* and *Inner Security and Infinite Wealth*

Don't Fix Me, I'm not Broken

Changing Our Minds About Ourselves
and Our Children

Don't Fix Me, I'm not Broken

Changing Our Minds About Ourselves and Our Children

Sally Patton

BOOKS

Winchester, UK
Washington, USA

First published by O-Books, 2011
O-Books is an imprint of John Hunt Publishing Ltd., Laurel House, Station Approach,
Alresford, Hants, SO24 9JH, UK
office1@o-books.net
www.o-books.com

For distributor details and how to order please visit the 'Ordering' section on our website.

Text copyright: Sally Patton 2010

ISBN: 978 1 84694 466 6

Design: Tom Davies

Printed in the UK by CPI Antony Rowe
Printed in the USA by Offset Paperback Mfrs, Inc

We operate a distinctive and ethical publishing philosophy in all
areas of our business, from our global network of authors to
production and worldwide distribution.

CONTENTS

About the Author

Sally Patton has advocated and worked for children labeled as disabled for over 35 years. She conducts spiritual workshops for adults focused on raising and ministering to children, particularly children with special needs.

Sally's journey began when her son was labeled as 'severely dyslexic', leaving her feeling like she was in a 'desert of no beginnings and no endings'. Desperate to get out, she embarked on a spiritual quest that nurtured her own healing, leading to an awareness that it was not her son she had to change, but herself. From a place of despair she learned to embrace the wonder in her own son. She realized that it is not about fixing her son, or anyone else, it is about changing our minds to see with the eyes of love instead of fear.

She teaches this journey of hope and healing at her workshops and through personal consultations.

Sally has a Masters of Education degree and with her faith in the spiritual journey of life, she teaches how parenting a child with a special needs label can be a spiritual journey of blessings and healing, and how this means trusting and letting go of judgments.

She runs workshops for parents and caregivers on learning to walk lightly while parenting children with special needs. Looking beyond the labels and seeing the divine in each child.

She offers personal consultations for individuals to **explore parenting or caregiving of children with special needs from a spiritual perspective, with a focus on tapping into our own inner knowing and healing through forgiveness.**

She also runs workshops for faith communities on radical hospitality as a spiritual practice for ministers and religious educators, to encourage the weaving of all children into the congregation, creating moments of transcendence, and teaching proactive techniques for behavior management.

Sally Patton is the author of *Welcoming Children with Special Needs: A Guidebook for Faith Communities*.

To order call UUA Bookstore at 1-800-215-9076.

Her inspirational website is www.embracechildspirit.org

Foreword

For too long the focus has been on how to fix the child. Yet real healing begins with the parents and caregivers. At last, here is a book that reorders our perception of caring for children with a so called challenging condition or situation by asking us to look into the mirror at our own uninvestigated beliefs and fears. This is a book that can lead you out of desperation and into liberation. From emotional imprisonment to spiritual awakening, if you have the courage to begin the journey by asking one question...

Having survived the traumatic experience of almost losing our teenage daughter through deep depression, anorexia and bulimia, I was excited to discuss with Sally Patton the idea of her writing this essential book. 'Don't Fix Me, I'm Not Broken' was born from Sally's own experience, both personal and professional. We believe that this book will encourage many parents to totally re-evaluate and therefore transform both their own parenting experience and that of their children's as well.

Life with a child who is undergoing a challenging condition can often be experienced as a nightmare. But the anguish is unknowingly intensified and reinforced when we journey through it with fear and doubt as our guides. If we can learn to use our children's situation or condition as a catalyst for facing up to and *undoing* fear rather than feeding it, both parent and child can unite in healing the underlying cause of all distress – which is fear itself. When the perception of fear falls away all that's left is love. Love is the core of our true nature. Unfortunately, we are much more familiar with fear than with love and as such, we unconsciously attract whatever we fear.

As parents it took us a while to learn that the purpose of our life was not to acquire what we believed we lacked in our lives or to fix those people and things we believed were broken. It took many heartbreaking events before we realized that our true life purpose was to *un*learn all the beliefs and values that blocked our awareness of love within and without.

Most of us in this world unknowingly operate from a false-self (ego) that has fear and deprivation at its center. While this perception runs our life we will not know real love, peace and joy. Parenting our own sick child for three years was an opportunity to undo a large mass of our mistaken beliefs and values, all founded upon fear and not on love as we previously believed. Little did we know that our daughter's illness would be the greatest catalyst for healing our own conscious and unconscious fears. Through learning to listen and focus on the ever-present (but not always visible!) love that lay at our daughters core (and thus at our own core) we gradually came to realize that what we focused on grew – considerably. And by not giving false power to her disability and illness, it eventually faded into the background until one day, it was gone forever.

Don't Fix Me, I'm Not Broken' is an extraordinarily helpful book. It is unique in its approach and aim. It asks us to open ourselves to the deeper meaning behind our children's seeming condition. It invites us to be willing to renounce our human story about this condition and to ask the Divine to reveal the lessons of love that await our welcome. *"I see **you**, not the behavior, not the condition or the label; I see the truth of you."*

This is a statement of unconditional regard; it is not achieved through intellectual understanding alone but by experience. Extending unconditional regard for our children does not mean excusing bad behavior or shirking responsibility but it does mean choosing to see *beyond* the physical, beyond the labels – body, behavior, emotions or mental health, to the source of love that beckons a witness to bring it forth both in our child's experience and our own. Our children bring to us the gift of Life, which is the reminder of the true goal of all our relationships, to heal our sense of separation from ourselves, each other and God.

Sally Patton helps us to recognize the fundamental issue that blocks healing with our children. The issue is revealed in the form of one question – one that only *you* can answer. This question is critical and yet is so often overlooked by parents – *"are you parenting from fear or from love?"*

Sally introduces this valuable question in myriad forms throughout her book. When we can, through honest self-inquiry, source the *intent* from which we parent, we've made headway and opened the door to love. Healing of our perception can now occur and because all minds are joined, healing in our child can now take place as well. By staying vigilant through learning to ask this question as often as our peace appears to be threatened by fear, anger, frustration, etc, we will emerge as the parents and caregivers we always wanted to be and develop lasting, unbreakable bonds of gratitude and love with our children, ourselves and God.

We wish you an enlightening read of this most valuable book. But most of all, our desire is that you decide to *apply* the healing principles you encounter within the following pages. Allow yourself to engage in the transformative power of love, a power that will restore to you a sense of wholeness, wellbeing, connection and peace.

Nouk Sanchez and Tomas Vieira
authors of *Take Me to Truth; Undoing the Ego*

www.TakeMeToTruth.com

Preface

Remember, any encounter with your child is a holy encounter, especially those moments that push us into the depths of despair. It is how we choose to ultimately handle those moments that either mires us in the "why me" syndrome or sets us free. There is always a blessing in every difficult or challenging situation. It may take awhile to see. You may desperately want to feel it immediately. Trust it will come. If you expect it, you will find it, and sorrow will turn to joy. If you ask, the Unified Spirit will show you the way.

I wrote those words for an email bulletin I was sending to parents who had attended one of my workshops. It took a long time for me to come to a place of peace. In retrospect it feels like a miraculous journey, but while I was in the midst of it, it often felt too hard and too painful.

I started this journey of parenting a child with a special needs label thinking this was a problem to be solved. Thinking that if I just looked long and hard enough, I could fix his problem. I was most definitely stuck in the "why did this have to happen to me?" state of mind, and the medical model of treatment that posits that when there is something wrong with your child, you fix him or her. At some point I had a very small glimmer of realization that maybe it was not my son who had to change, but me. This realization launched me on one of those journeys where I embraced all the new thought spiritual teachings that came my way. I definitely took the smorgasbord approach to my assertions that "There has to be a better way to live, to parent my children, to be in relationship with my spouse."Ultimately it was the process of parenting a child whom the world viewed as defective that changed me and set me free.

What I think all of us want as parents is to be able to parent from a place of peace, no matter what is happening around us, no matter what struggles our children are having. What many spiritual teachings emphasize, and I have come to realize, is that peace lies within, that all problems and all solutions to problems come from within. The daily chores and activities of parenting any child can pull us out of peace. However, it is often our child with a label or a child who is struggling or defiant, who challenges us the most, as we are confronted on a daily basis with the difficulties associated with our children's disorder, disability, or defiance.

Seeing our child as different, more difficult, more challenging, having 'special needs', is reinforced by a world focused on seeing some people as more damaged or less normal than others, and then trying to fix them. I came to realize it is not about controlling or fixing our children; it is about changing our minds about our children. And when we do this, we find a universal truth for healing all relationships. The catalyst for my journey may have been my son, but what I discovered was a path of forgiveness for all aspects of my life.

We can always choose peace instead of what we are experiencing.[1] I find images of water help when I want to access the place of peace that always exists within. I am reminded of some lines from the song,

Peace I ask of thee, oh river
Peace, peace, peace
When I learn to live serenely
Cares will cease

I am sure this is a familiar camp song for many of you. I spent summers singing this song. I love the soothing music and the harmony. I was content and at peace as a child lazily floating the rivers in the hills of the Ozarks. I have spent most of my adult years thinking inner peace was not possible. I was constantly grieving over past mistakes or worrying about the future. I forgot what it was like to float down the river on a sunny day, singing songs with friends or just being quiet and still and listening to the birds and bugs and watching the trees pass by. It was easy to float with the current of the river, let go of all thoughts, and just be in the moment.

Inner peace often feels impossible while parenting a child with multiple needs, especially a child who does not seem to go with your flow, who challenges us and constantly disrupts our ability to stay calm. We allow their struggles to become like the rocks in the path of a river. Instead of being like the water flowing around these rocks, we are like the sticks and the flotsam that get stuck on the rocks till something dislodges us or the water gradually wears down resistance so we once again join the flow of the river, the spiritual flow of life. Can we be as the Taoist proverb suggests?

The highest motive in life is to be like water. It fights nothing or no one. It flows to and from its source and in the flowing smoothes and wears away all resistance.

Do we have the courage to be with our child and let go of all the pain, the worry, and the fear? Can we have the courage to say to ourselves...

Our child is defiant and will not listen – it just is.
Our child exhibits bizarre behavior – it just is.
Our child is isolated and uncommunicative – it just is.
Our child has to have another operation – it just is.
Our child cannot hear – it just is.
Our child cannot see – it just is.
Our child cannot walk – it just is.
Our child struggles to read – it just is.
Our child has cognitive limitations – it just is.
Our child rages and fights life – it just is.
Our child is deeply depressed and cuts – it just is.

Our child is addicted to alcohol or drugs – it just is.
Our child is suicidal – it just is.

I can imagine a collective gasp as people read these statements of acceptance, especially the last one, yet it is all about the ability to be at peace while your child is falling apart. This does not mean we give up caring and parenting. This does not mean we stop guiding and advocating for our children. It means we accept the flow of spirit in our life and stop trying to control the current. We trust the Unified Spirit, God's voice of oneness in this world, as it works through us and through our children. And when we surrender to the spiritual current within us, it all becomes easier; we regain the stately calm within, the pieces fall into place, the people we need to help our children appear, our children stop fighting us so much. We notice the blessings in our life, we accept what is.

Accepting what is means realizing that it is the beliefs and the story we create around our child's disability, disorder, or disease that causes unhappiness or grief, not the disorder or disability implied by the label. 'My child is autistic, dyslexic, bipolar, attention-deficit disordered, physically disabled, cognitively limited, depressed and drug-addicted...' are all just thoughts. We can either buy into the traditional stories about these labels or we can choose peace instead. As parents of children with labels or any child who is struggling or just being every-day difficult, we can either embrace this opportunity for our own spiritual growth or we can stay stuck in the anger, pain, and the sadness. It is our choice.

Introduction

If I smile and don't believe
Soon I know I'll wake from this dream
Don't try to fix me, I'm not broken.
-Evanescence, *Hello, from* Fallen

This is not a book on specific spiritual parenting techniques. This is a book about questioning our beliefs and our thoughts concerning what it means to be a parent and what our expectations are for our children. Too often we allow our happiness to be determined by how our children are doing. We decide that in order to be happy and fulfilled, our children need to be good athletes, or good students, or artistic, or good at something. They need to have friends, they need to behave in a certain way, they need to show respect to adults, they need to be more independent, or they need to show their love more, they need to be normal — whatever that means to us — they need to be this or that for us to be happy. If they do all of this, then we will be happy.

We decide that when our children are happy, we will be happy. But when we do this, we've decided happiness lies outside of us, that someone else is responsible for our happiness instead of ourselves. When we make the decision to own our children's life stories, it is a set-up for failure, because happiness lies within us, not outside of us.

If our spiritual questioning and inquiry leads us to parent from a place of unconditional love, joy, and peace, no matter what is happening to our child, then that is the most empowering teaching experience we can model for our children. This does not mean we give up the daily advocating, teaching, and guiding of our children, it means we now do it from a place of unconditional love and peace.

Often it is a child born with a physical or cognitive limitation, or one who struggles emotionally or educationally, or a child who becomes disabled through an accident, who compels us to question our relationship with God or to ask how God could let this happen. Certainly this happened to me and helped fuel my spiritual journey. Eventually all my searching, meditating, studying, praying to the Goddess, and questioning my beliefs led me to *A Course in Miracles (ACIM)* which informs the writing of this book.

I understand now that the Unified Spirit (God's voice in this world) was gently guiding me to approaches and symbols that I could understand at the time. So while they may not represent the absolute truth, they are ideas and techniques that helped me along the path to understanding and that I share with you in this book. I hope they will help you on your chosen spiritual path. For those who are students of *A Course in Miracles*, and for those who want to learn more, there is further discussion from *A Course in Miracles* perspective at the end of the book.

I will use the following terms and definitions throughout the book.

God – the source of infinite spiritual intelligence, an experience that transcends anything on earth, changeless, formless, eternal love and pure spirit.

Unified Spirit – God's voice of unconditional love in this world signifying we are all one in spirit, our unified higher self. Depending on your spiritual path you may want to substitute with the Holy Spirit, Jesus, the Buddha or another spiritual master.

Ego – the thought of separation from our Source which creates fear and manifests as the constant stream of involuntary and compulsive thinking of the past and the future leading to judgment of ourselves and others; a false sense of self.

Level of Form – this physical existence, the physical body, the ego-self.

Level of Spirit – our spiritual connection and oneness with God.

Forgiveness – Seeing people with the eyes of love, without judgment, healing our thoughts of separation.

Because our children, especially those with labels, are often the source of immense tension, guilt, and fear, as well as overwhelming love in families, our relationship with them provides a perfect spiritual classroom for healing our thoughts of separation from others, and thus, God. In a sense, our children with labels represent the ultimate in fear and judgment. Not only are they separate bodies, as are all of us; they are perceived as defective separate bodies. Given the unremitting pressure by health and psychological or educational professionals, as well as by family and friends, to see our children as damaged, it takes enormous courage to perceive them differently.

The greatest gift we can give our children is to see the divine light in them no matter what is happening for them physically and emotionally. And if our children can not readily access their divine light, then it is our job to hold it for them until they can. Really it is as simple as that, conveying to our child, "I see you, not the label, not the behavior; I see the truth of you." All the parenting techniques in the world are ineffective without this attitude of positive, unconditional regard for your child.

Within this spiritual classroom, I was guided to ideas and teaching tools to help along the path toward awareness and forgiveness. These ideas may not be the absolute truth, however they help with understanding.

It helps to see our lives as spiritual classrooms. When we embrace this idea we can look at ways to see beyond the label to the wholeness of spirit in every child so we do not give power to the label.

We will discuss ways to recognize that people are always doing the best they can with the knowledge and awareness they have in each moment. We will explore the idea we always have a choice and by changing our thoughts we change our story and experience of our labeled children from one of struggle and sadness to one of joy and peace. And we will explore the idea that all of us are whole spiritual beings. Each of us has our own unique path to follow. This involves accepting what is, trusting, letting go of fear and surrendering to the Unified Spirit's plan for us and our children.

Chapter I

Parenting Our Labeled Children, a Difficult Spiritual Classroom

Never, ever forget that you have been chosen for this very special journey. It matters not what the challenges may be; what matters is that you open your heart to this child. For as difficult as things may get, you will discover that this soul, wrapped in this precious little package, has much to give and volumes to teach you about yourself — if you are willing to learn.

–Trena Tremblay, *You Will Dream New Dreams*

Being able to accept that we are in a spiritual classroom makes a profound difference in our ability to be at peace while parenting. We chose to be on this journey with our children, even those who are seen as different, disabled, or disordered. Choosing to believe we are in a spiritual classroom where every experience is a spiritual lesson, is freeing. It allows us to trust that there is a light at the end of every dark tunnel. It helps us to look for the blessings and expect they are there, even when we cannot see them immediately. It helps us learn to love what is.

If we choose God's voice of oneness in this physical world as our teacher, rather than being ruled by the ego's thought system of fear, then we can begin to trust that every event or person in our lives is here to help us learn. The circumstances may not change, but our perceptions change. Our life becomes a miraculous journey of understanding rather than a life to be endured or a series of obstacles to overcome.

To begin our spiritual parenting journey, it is helpful to have some initial familiarity with the concepts of ego, forgiveness, and the physical and spiritual levels that are used in this book and are briefly defined in the Introduction. The purpose of this book is to help us gain a deeper understanding of these concepts within the framework of parenting.

The ego of spiritual teachings is not the ego of psychology, which is viewed as a positive and necessary development in a child. There are some similarities with the idea of "I" as a separate person from everyone else. The ego is a false sense of self resulting from our feelings of disconnection from God, other people and our deeper being. The basic emotion of the ego is fear. The ego's creation is the result of our belief in separation from the Source, which is God. Our reality is oneness with God so this belief in separation is a mistake. This mistake leads us to believe we are separate from others. Eckhart Tolle, a spiritual teacher promoting living only in the present, says that the ego manifests as the incessant stream of involuntary and compulsive thinking of the past and future. This compulsive thinking is always about judging ourselves and others.

I use the concept of the ego consistently in this book as the thoughts that prevent us from remembering our spiritual truth, our oneness with God. Our ego-self only wants us to believe we are physical bodies and thus are not pure spirit at one with our Source. Thus we often exist on two levels, this physical body, which is supported by our ego-self, and our spiritual self, which remembers our oneness with God.

The act of forgiving our thoughts of separation without judgment of ourselves and others is what undoes the ego and allows us to wake up and remember we are one with God. *A Course in Miracles* and other spiritual paths, such as Buddhism, suggest that we are dreaming this physical existence. I talk more about this in the final chapter; however it is not necessary to believe this is all a dream in order to grasp that we exist on two levels with two teachers. The ego keeps us believing we are physical bodies and the Unified Spirit reminds us that we are pure spirit. Forgiveness is being able to see absolutely everyone with the eyes of God's unconditional love, recognizing that everyone, without exception, is pure spirit no matter how they are acting in their physical bodies.

I will come back to this concept of the ego and forgiveness over and over again and will explain it in many different ways, so do not worry if it still does not make sense to you at this time. It is all a process of understanding that we are in a spiritual classroom composed of many lessons to help us gain a deeper understanding of these metaphysical truths. So long as I believe I am this physical body rather than pure spirit, I still have much to learn.

An understanding of being in a spiritual classroom did not come easily to me. When my husband and I began to realize that our son Tyler's learning- and information-processing difficulties were so severe that school professionals did not know what to do with him, we became absorbed by the ensuing fight with the public school system, and it became our life. I had fallen into the "poor me" trap. I can remember complaining to my mother how unfair it was, my brothers had the money to fight this, I did not. During most of this time my husband was unemployed and money was tight. I was mad at the schools, I was mad at the professionals working with Tyler, I was mad at my husband for being unemployed, I was mad at the rest of the world for not understanding what we were going through. After a year of fighting, I realized one day that I had totally isolated myself in pain and anger.

Some parents get so mired in fighting and caring for their child they begin to see their child as a burden or they just wish their child was "normal" so they could have the life they wanted. While certainly this is a normal and understandable response, it never happened to me. What I saw was this radiant child whom I felt everyone else was trying to destroy. But I can understand how it happens. Sometimes the needs of the child are so overwhelming and so continuous; parents feel they never have a break. Their entire life has been spent just coping. They are constantly advocating for their child, which often means fighting the professionals who usually cannot help, fighting the school system for appropriate educational services, and maybe fighting their spouse or partner, family, and friends about what to do. And if you are like me, I watched my child's radiance begin to fade as he began to comprehend all the negative messages implying he was defective in some way and not like "normal" children. I kept thinking, "How can this be? He's just a beautiful child."

I remember one particularly difficult meeting with our town's special education director. He asked what was wrong with our family that our six-year-old son could not read or write his name or address. It took many years before I forgave him. One mother of a child with cerebral palsy told me that when she was in the hospital with her baby, she read the social worker's report noting she was holding and hugging her baby way too much. These are just two examples of why parents develop armor and a readiness to do battle at all times. And we fall into the trap of thinking the problem is out there with all those people who do not understand, or that the problem is with our child's disorder, disability, or disease, or a combination of both.

The process of realizing I am always in a spiritual classroom was a long one. I can look back on my life and clearly see each step toward more clarity and understanding and how each event was a stepping stone to another event with even more understanding. It is difficult to see in the moment how each event and crisis allows us to be where we are now.

In this book I will describe many of the tools, techniques, and levels of awareness that helped me eventually parent from a place of peace. It did not happen all at once. Even now, I still can catch myself wanting to fix my children's problems or control what is happening in their lives. The Unified Spirit brought what I needed at the time, what I could accept, and continues to do this.

Eventually, through questioning my beliefs, I arrived at a place of calm that stayed, even when Tyler slid into deep depression and started cutting himself at age seventeen. I had finally learned, and was able to accept totally and completely, not to take on my son's pain. If we take on our children's pain or struggle, then what occurs is that you have two miserable people instead of one. We are demonstrating that our children's pain is more important than their wholeness of spirit. The best gift I could give my son at the time was to parent from a place of peace with an unshakable faith and trust in his ability to get through this with his spiritual self intact, no matter the outcome. I was able to maintain this calm even when he cut the words "help me" into his arm. And he did get through it and he regained his radiance.

Not taking on our children's story is the same whether our child has a label and struggles or our child fits into the cultural definition of normal. Many parents use their children's achievements to bolster their own self worth. My bright and lovely daughter Sarah was an early educational star and a gifted artist, which continued all the way through school and college. It was easy to be proud of her achievements. I was constantly catching myself bragging or comparing her to other children. I realized I was using her success to enhance my sense of worth.

We often want our children to succeed where we have not, to use their achievements to bolster our own self esteem. Taking on any child's story, whether they are traditionally successful or seen as defective with a label, is the same. We are giving power to a story. We believe our children are responsible for our happiness or unhappiness, which demonstrates that their actions and behavior define who they are. This teaches that their happiness is found outside of themselves rather than from within. By seeing past the label, the achievements, the behavior, and loving them no matter what, we are demonstrating their divine self is more important than their ego self.

Parenting and Unconditional Love

The psychologist Carl Rogers, who is now, unfortunately, somewhat out of favor in the psychology profession, developed a personality theory based on two main concepts: conditional positive regard and unconditional positive regard. Conditional positive regard is when you only value or love someone based on a certain acceptable way of behaving. This is parenting with the ego as your teacher. Many of us feel our parents' love was conditional based on what they needed in order to feel loved or respected. When we are parenting from the ego we are inclined to take credit for our child's successes and blame them for all their failures. You can imagine what this can do to a child's self esteem.

Because we are human, most of us parent from a combination of both conditional and unconditional positive regard. We are proud of our children's achievements, we sometimes judge their decisions, yet we still love them. When we get stuck in the past obsessing about, or relying upon how we were parented, then we slip into the ego thought system of conditional love. Many of us continue to parent with the beliefs we inherited from our parents. An example might be, parents are adults and therefore they are to be honored and obeyed no matter what; any questioning of decisions is disrespectful.

When we stay in presence, realizing our past child experiences are just thoughts repeating in the present, then we can release our parents' control as having any power to affect how we parent our children. Unconditional positive regard means loving someone unconditionally no matter their behavior. We can embrace the light of truth in every child without having to condone undesirable behavior on the level of this physical existence.

Unconditional positive regard is seeing people through the unconditional love of the Unified Spirit.

The fears we have for our labeled children can cripple us; fear chokes out love for ourselves, for others who are seen as different, and for people who are trying to help. Early on, when Tyler was in kindergarten and I realized what was happening, I thought 'I will fix this problem' because I believed, then, that fixing was the answer. I was motivated by fear for my son's well being and future. Yet it was a fear that took me out of peace into constant worry. When it was decided Tyler should repeat kindergarten and be placed in a classroom for special needs children, I thought, my goodness how can you flunk kindergarten?

The first day I took Tyler to the new kindergarten, we arrived and most of these beautiful children with their individual struggles were in distress; one girl in particular was crying and screaming uncontrollably. I left Tyler in tears to go to a job interview. Needless to say, I was so upset by Tyler's distress that the interview did not go well. I was not present as I let worry take over.

The day passed, Tyler settled into his new situation, and his ability to stay present and happy took over. The children in this special needs classroom learned empathy and kindness for each other that have stayed with Tyler to this day. While I could not see it at the time, it was a perfect experience for both of us. And this is what Tyler taught me, to stay present and not become consumed by fears and worry. This allows the learnings and blessings to occur. The only person harmed by my fear was me. It did not change the situation, it did not help Tyler, it only made the actual experience appear awful and the person who suffered was me. This was just the beginning of thinking that maybe there was a different way.

My journey took me from rejecting all organized religion to an absolute breathtaking period of intense spiritual wonder. I explored and read the books of all the spiritual teachers who appeared in my awareness from Neale Donald Walsh, Wayne Dyer, Deepak Chopra, Sonia Choquette, Caroline Myss, Starhawk, David Hawkins, Joseph Chilton Pearce, Barry Neal Kaufman, Eckhart Tolle, Byron Katie, to *A Course in Miracles* authors Gary Renard, Ken Wapnick, Gerald Jampolsky, and Nouk Sanchez and Tomas Vieira, to name just a few.

I combined this spiritual exploration with the exploration of learning disabilities in order to better understand Tyler. I attended all the conferences, workshops, and seminars held in the Boston area. Eventually I was led to focus on the spiritual side of parenting a child with a special-needs label. And throughout all of this, Tyler continued to teach just by being.

Once we accept being in a spiritual classroom, we realize we are all students and we also teach by just being who we are. The mistake parents often make is to believe only they are the teachers and their children are the students. In actuality, we learn from each other. Obviously parents have more life experience and must provide support and guidance, but we miss opportunities for growth if we think our only job is to teach our children. We learn and teach in all of our relationships. What matters is whether we choose the ego or the Unified Spirit for our teacher, in other words, whether we choose fear or unconditional love. Those moments with our children (or with anybody), which are fraught with tension, stress, and resistance to accepting what is, provide our greatest learning opportunities.

When someone upsets me or pushes my buttons, I know it is time to look inward. We like to believe that the reason we are upset is because of something someone did, but this is not the case. The same things that upset me are not necessarily going to be the same things that upset you. Ask yourself why, it has to be something inside us that needs to be healed.

Understanding that we project onto other people our inner fears, dislikes, and problems can be difficult to accept. We want to believe we are right and everyone else is wrong. We all do this.

The ego has a need to be right. That's how arguments start; I am right and you are wrong.

We do this with our children under the guise of parenting. I am older, wiser, and you will do what I say. If you are constantly fighting your child about something, then it is time to go inward and examine why the event that triggered the fight is so upsetting. This feels so much more difficult if your child rages at life and becomes physically out of control.

How can the struggle associated with my child's disability or disorder possibly be an outcome of my inward condition? How can I possibly experience peace when my child has to have another operation, or more chemotherapy, or is nonverbal and sometimes violent? You can add your own scenario. We can get stuck on this question when we live in fear about what will happen to our child. I know well–intentioned, loving parents who have tried absolutely everything to control their child's disruptive or distressing behavior. The operative word here is control. We cannot control anyone else. We are only responsible for ourselves. So if this is the case, what do we do about an out-of-control child, or a child strung out on drugs or alcohol, or self abusing, or any number of destructive behaviors or debilitating diseases or accidents? The worries start and we can feel desperate and sometimes we hate our child or become overwhelmed with worry.

What is needed is a change in perspective. We cannot control or change a situation, we can only change how we view a situation. When we realize the situation is an opportunity for a spiritual lesson, then we release the need to control and the space is created for our child's inner spiritual voice to be heard, and healing can begin.

I remember reading a wonderful story about changing one's perspective from spiritual teachers and ministers Hugh and Gayle Prather in their book, *Spiritual Parenting*, which is now out of print. Their son provided a continual challenge to their parenting skills. At one point they even confessed they did not like him much because parenting was a constant battle. They decided to pray about it. Prayer for the Prathers involved stilling their minds and letting go of any opinion as to what they think is the problem. Out of prayer they determined to accept their son completely. They set aside two sacred periods a day in which they would come together to picture their son in the light of God and silently speak to him from their hearts.

After several weeks of this practice they had a breakthrough. "Suddenly we began to see *Jordan*. And he was a wonderful kid! We began noticing his exuberance, his insightfulness, his offbeat creativity and inventiveness, his delightful sense of humor, his mental toughness and centeredness, and many other qualities that we had been blind to – merely because he didn't share the easygoing personalities that the rest of us had. Jordan has never been one to suffer in silence, but we saw that this was actually a good balance to have in our family. We needed Jordan. We needed his directness. It was no accident that he was in our lives."[2] With their change in perspective the Prathers were able to relax and enjoy their son's differences. Trying to change Jordan had only caused them to see the worse in him. When they changed their perspective their son also changed in a positive way.

Seeing the World through a Child's Eyes

I talk a lot in my workshops about seeing the world through a child's eyes, whether it is your own child or someone else's. When we see life through a child's eyes, we realize a common bond of experiencing the world in the same way, only the form of our actions is different. This is part of being in a spiritual classroom, recognizing everyone is always doing the best they can with the information and awareness they have in the moment. (I will discuss this more thoroughly in Chapter four.) Understanding this often comes from being able to see the world from a child's perspective. Dr Robert Brooks in *Raising Resilient Children,* calls this empathy. To me, empathy is reminding myself that this person or child who is pushing my buttons is doing the best he or she can. I remember their behavior is not who they are, that the divine flame exits in them.

Gerald Jampolsky, a psychiatrist and *A Course in Miracles* teacher, uses the symbol of a lamp shade as the ego that covers our divine light.[3] I think some of our labeled children have layers of dark lamp shades covering their radiance. Our job is to always remember the radiance is there, it never disappears. We remove the lampshades with our love. Love unifies us. It changes an impossible situation and brings peace. However, it can only work if we let go of the past and release any investment in outcome. When we have need for a certain outcome, then once again we have given away our power to be happy. The outcome becomes more important than unconditional love.

Tantrums, complaining, and annoying behavior are very common among small children, so I use them as small examples of how we can change our minds about a situation and have peace instead. The principle is the same whether our child has a tantrum or engages in harmful behavior or has a debilitating disease — whatever the perceived problem. When our children have tantrums, the first thing we do is review in our mind all the times in the past when our child raged. The response is to go immediately into fear of what will happen based on our past experience. Once in fear we respond automatically with threats or begging, or trying to reason which did not work before and will probably not work again. And if this tantrum happens in public, then we exacerbate the problem by worrying that other people see us as incompetent parents.

A typical scenario for parents is, a young child sees something he or she wants while shopping. We tell the child that he or she cannot have it and a tantrum or crying and begging ensues. The first thing to do is to see the situation through your child's eyes.

I want lots of things while I shop and I often convince myself that if I can just have such and such item, I will feel good or look beautiful. It is how marketing works. We believe the object of our desire will make us happy. I will look beautiful and sophisticated in a certain dress and therefore will be happy.

Our children learn at a very young age to believe someone else or something else is responsible for their happiness. We could not have set up a better situation for perpetuating the belief we need someone else to be happy. The baby is helpless, so when in distress, he has to cry in order to be fed or have his diaper changed. Someone else is responsible for his happiness. He has learned that crying and having tantrums get a response and his needs are met.

Other events that often push parents' buttons center on taking care of one's belongings and cleaning up messes. I remember a long-standing struggle I had with my children about hanging up their coats when they came home from school or day care. There are hooks by the back door for this purpose. Yet every night I would find their coats on the floor. No amount of suggesting or pleading seemed to make a difference. It annoyed me so much I started to make it into more and more of an issue and the harder I pushed, the more my children resisted.

Finally one day I realized it was not worth fighting over, I let go and began to see the humor in the situation. I began to look at it from my children's perspective. Coats on the floor are not very important, Mom is being absurd. Once the resistance was gone, I made a joke about the coats on the floor that the kids laughed about. The next day, I made an observation without any anger, "The coats are on the floor." From then on the children voluntarily hung their coats on the hooks by the back door without any reminders from me. A large part of releasing resistance to annoying events is seeing it through other's eyes and then seeing the humor in the situation. Then we can observe without the anger attached. When we can laugh in painful times, it means we are beginning to release our resistance to loving what is.

Just recently I was walking in the woods behind our house, following a grandmother and her two young grandchildren. The boy was content holding his grandmother's hand; however, the girl was lagging behind, complaining about the bugs and being itchy. The grandmother had tried reasoning and engaging the girl in noticing the beauty of the forest. Nothing worked. As I walked closer, the grandmother started telling the girl it was not nice to always be complaining, that no one likes a complainer. As I passed and smiled and said good morning, the grandmother smiled apologetically, and then I heard her say to her grand-daughter, "I am sorry you itch; I should have put some bug spray on you before we left." It was like turning a switch; the little girl stopped complaining and started being interested in where they were walking.

My assessment of the situation is that with my friendly greeting the grandmother realized how she was responding and then acknowledged her granddaughter was upset. When our children complain, often the first response is to discount what they are saying and ask them to stop. Sometimes all we need to do is let our children know they have been heard.

While it may not always be possible in a public place to totally let go of the fear and see the situation through your child's eyes and eventually the eyes of love, with practice, it will happen. Love fills the present moment when you release thinking about what happened in the past, worrying about what other people are thinking, and worrying that these tantrums or complaints will occur every time you go to the store or take a walk. It may not happen immediately, but it will come.

The process of changing how we perceive the events in our lives is the same, whether it is a stubbed toe, a child's tantrum, or a life-threatening event. On the level of form in this physical world, one event feels bigger, more important, and more painful than another event. On the level of spirit, it is all the same, we release the fear in order for love to enter, which allows us to parent from that stately calm within.

Letting Go of Fear and Letting Love In

Letting go of fear is the most important lesson we learn in this spiritual classroom. I hear parents say, "This will not work, my child's disability, disorder, disease is too severe." "There are just some life events where no amount of attitude change will release the pain I feel." "You cannot possibly understand what I am going through because you have never experienced it." This is the ego talking. It does not want you to find peace in all this trauma and pain. Yet isn't peace what we truly want, to be calm, no matter what is happening around us? Why would we want to give the power to make us miserable to any event or person in our lives? Does being miserable or upset or sad or angry change the situation? Wouldn't the struggling people around us benefit from our calmness and joy?

Fear manifests itself when we let in the past, and worry about the future. I know some parents feel they have to worry about the future because their son or daughter will not be able to take care of themselves. There is a difference between planning for your child's future and constantly worrying about it. The worry does not solve the problems, calmness presents solutions. And being present, not obsessing about the past, or worrying about the future, allows life to unfold with grace. With the love and awareness that your child is safe on the level of spirit, you will be guided by the Unified Spirit about what to do.

Another ego trap is to be invested in the outcome. We can say to ourselves we will trust there are blessings in every painful struggle; however, most of us make our inner peace conditional on a preconceived outcome. My son must learn to talk. My daughter must stop hitting me. My son must stop using drugs. This even applies to the hard one, my child must live. This is where we start to bargain. It feels like a paradox to completely let go of any need to control the outcome in order for fear to leave and love and peace to enter. It feels like falling off a cliff. Trust the Unified Spirit is there to catch you and float you gently home to God. And as we learn to replace fear with love in the moment, we will model for our children that peace and happiness come from inside not from an object or person. When we let go and completely trust in God then our children feel the release and also change.

In this spiritual classroom we recognize our children are our teachers. Their tantrum or annoying habit becomes our lesson. The situation may not change but our perceptions and attitude change so we know without question, "I could see peace instead of this."[4] And in my experience, your child feels this change and his or her behavior will change.

I have a visualization that helps in understanding how letting go of resistance changes the actions of the people involved. I visualize the person whom I think is annoying, taking a swing at me. When they hit me, I experience pain and I want to attack back. When there is no resistance, there is nothing to hit, they take a swing and hit nothing, just air, because there is nothing there. There is no point in continuing with behavior that receives no reinforcement.

Sometimes I come across a sentence, phrase, poem, or song that speaks eloquently to what I am experiencing or learning. Often it will spark an entire essay, which I share via an email newsletter. I have found that the Unified Spirit provides what I need to learn in this classroom called life. I will be led to buy books that speak immediately to where I am in my level of awareness. Sometimes I buy a book or read an article that absolutely has no meaning for me only to later read it with a profound learning.

When we are ready, we are guided to what we can understand. This is another way to realize we are always doing the best we can with the information and awareness we have in the moment. In the next moment my awareness changes and the words or life event take on new meaning. It is a living, changing process and the spiral is always upward in this spiritual classroom.

The following words from *The Telling* by Ursula K. Le Guin, express what I feel about being in this spiritual classroom.

When my guides lead me in Kindness
I follow, follow lightly,
And there are no footprints
in the dust behind us.[5]

I love this quote. It expresses how I feel about turning over my physical life journey to the Unified Spirit to lead in kindness; trusting that as I follow lightly I will not leave any permanent footprints in this life's drama to fuel the belief in separation from the Source.

Recently a friend of Tyler's died from a combination of alcohol and drugs in Laos, Asia, far from his home. Jack was a high-energy child always testing boundaries, a different learner, warmhearted, highly creative, curious, and a risk taker. Jack also struggled with depression. Over Jack's short life I admired the love, flexibility, and humor his parents maintained in relation to their son. By the time Jack died at age 21, he had visited more than 40 countries on five continents. His love for excitement and his battle with depression led him to risky behavior and his death.

There are some people who would question Jack's parents for allowing the pursuit of his dream of exploration at such a young age, especially given his tendency toward risky behavior. It takes tremendous courage to trust and allow your child to follow his own path. On the level of form in this physical world, his death feels sad and hard. On the level of spirit, we know that Jack's life is part of the whole living process toward forgiveness — seeing all life through God's nonjudgmental, loving eyes. We cannot begin to understand the forgiveness lessons for Jack and his family. We can only trust that each and every one of us is part of the whole. We can only trust the Unified Spirit's plan for all of us, no matter the outcome.

Every moment is a perfect time to let go of the past, renew and parent from the stately calm within. I wish for everyone the will to connect with our guides, the Unified Spirit, our higher unified self to stay the course. Standing in your truth and allowing others to stand in theirs is important. Like Tyler and Jack, our children have their own path to truth; we cannot presume to know what it is. All we can do is support and create an environment that allows the discovery of their truth. Not judging our children's path comes from not judging ourselves. This, above all else, feels the most difficult, not judging someone else's path, especially when it feels harmful or alien to our beliefs.

"Learning to walk lightly" means letting go of judgments. When we let go of judgments we leave no foot prints. In other words we do not reinforce our belief in separation from God. Trust means letting go of our ego and releasing to a higher purpose we cannot begin to comprehend. Trusting our children will find and stand in truth at times takes immense courage, especially as with Jack it led to death at a young age. Trust and letting go of judgments and forgiving is what allows God's love to flow through us. In the end, this is the only way to get through the bad times to joy and inner peace. And in this spiritual classroom, we must be willing to do it over and over again. Inner peace comes from letting go, learning to walk lightly, and leave no foot prints.

Chapter II

No Child is a Mistake,
Seeing Past the Labels to the Spirit Within

*Let us hold always, this picture of our child in her completeness,
even especially in the face of those who see her as decomposed, a
collection of deficits.*
–Barbara Gill, *Changed By a Child*

No child is a mistake? What does this mean? We know in our
hearts that no child is a mistake, but when involved with a struggling child, we question if the disability, disorder, or difficult
behavior is a mistake. What does this mean when a mother gives
birth to a child with cognitive limitations or cerebral palsy? What
does this mean when a child is in an accident and becomes
seriously physically impaired? What does this mean when our
schools increasingly teach to standardized tests at the expense of
creative learning and all those children who learn differently?
What does this mean when more and more children are born
within the autism spectrum? The list could go on and on.

That question was asked by a mother attending one of my
workshops on spiritual parenting. She arrived angry and spent
much of the workshop crying. Her son Tim was six and had
cerebral palsy. She described him lovingly as full of energy and
a dynamo on wheels. Tim sometimes involuntarily jerks his
hands and his body, as do many people with cerebral palsy.

The mother had just received in the mail a Xerox copy
picturing the front of Tim's teacher's chest which showed a large
red stain on her white shirt. The note scribbled on the bottom
from the Principal said that Tim's behavior was highly

unacceptable and would not be tolerated. Evidently as the result of an involuntary spasm Tim had knocked the juice cup from his teacher's hands which spilled on her blouse. She immediately assumed he had done it on purpose and he was punished.

All of us in the workshop sat in stunned silence which eventually erupted into immense anger and an outpouring of stories of adults who do not see children as children but see only what is wrong with them. Now none of us in that room believed Tim was a mistake, especially his Mom. But there was a huge question as to why Tim and children like him have to struggle so with a disability as well as cope with other people's misunder-standings and prejudices.

Culturally we are taught that all of us are physical beings and some of us have a spiritual experience either alone or as part of a faith tradition. Many of us on a spiritual journey begin to realize that the opposite is true. We are spiritual beings having a physical experience. And because we are spiritual beings we are perfect in God's eyes. When we can see the divine spirit within every one of us, then we see that no one is a mistake. One of the ways to recognize the pure spirit in our children is to see past the labels and not give power to the label. How we do this when most people see the label and the deficits implied by the label is one of the lessons of being in a spiritual classroom.

As parents we need to find a way to do what we have to do to get needed services for our child without buying into the current cultural belief system about our child's diagnosis. I found one of the most effective ways to begin this process is to examine what it means to label our children and explore ways we can avoid the cultural game of labeling. Through this process we gain an understanding of how labeling keeps us believing our children are defective and in need of being fixed. Eventually we will be able to accept what is and not buy into the prevalent belief system about our child based on the label.

It is useful to recognize that a label is a label whether it is positive or negative. All labels come with expectations. Even the gifted or smart label can be just as limiting as a special needs label. These children must live up to the expectations implied by the label or they risk disappointing themselves and their parents and teachers. Parents easily get caught up in deciding that their child's success reflects on them and therefore will push the over-achieving child even harder. I have found some parents are much more forgiving and flexible with their child with a special needs label than with their child who is gifted in culturally approved ways. All the parents' wishes, dreams, and needs get transferred to the child who is perceived as "normal" or "gifted." We can begin to recognize the label and the expectations implied by the label and we can begin releasing the thoughts that surround a label. Too many children believe their actions, such as good grades, or being a good athlete or musician, defines who they are, so when they fail, they experience intense pain and unhappiness. Our job as parents is to stay in peace and model that happiness comes from within.

Children with Spiritual Labels

When Tyler was eight or nine years old, I can remember a conversation about reincarnation prompted by a storybook describing a person who had reincarnated as a cat. Tyler had a deep knowing of having lived past lives; he just could not understand why he would choose to come back as a child with a learning disability. I was totally caught unaware by his question and I think I mumbled something about Tyler having a strong soul.

Tyler's gentle radiant spirit was evident the day he was born. Children and adults were attracted to his brightness. He would attend a gathering whether it was for an adult or child and just be and people would come and talk to him without any effort on Tyler's part. I remember one particular social gathering when Tyler was seven and our daughter was at summer camp. Rick and I knew very few people and as introverts we always struggle with meeting new people and making conversation. Tyler calmly wandered off by himself and got some food and sat down at an empty table. Soon the table was full of adults all talking with Tyler just enjoying being in his presence.

Even during the many years of sliding into depression, Tyler's spiritual light was never totally obscured; it would still shine through and attract the people he needed to help him cope. Once he was ready to remove the darkness dimming his light, he rediscovered that just by being in radiance he attracted people who wanted to be with him.

Many years ago when Tyler was still young, I attended a conference about learning disabilities and a total stranger turned to me and asked if my son was spiritual and then she said I would write a book about it one day. Those simple words spoke a truth that has stayed with me and of course her prediction has come true. All of this eventually led me to wondering if Tyler was an "indigo" child.

The belief that there are some children called "indigo" or "crystal" children with special extra sensory abilities and a spiritual knowing has come out of the new thought spirituality movement. It has gained momentum and spawned many books about how to parent these children. According to some spiritual teachers, the "indigo" children were the first wave of children to reincarnate more spiritually aware. The "crystal" children are the next generation of children who are more psychically gifted.

Tyler is considered an "indigo" child by many people who know him. I spent some time researching "indigo" children and certainly came to the conclusion that Tyler had many of the characteristics and attributes of an "indigo" child. At the time, I liked the label much more than the learning disabled or dyslexic label. It implied something positive and spiritually special about Tyler, so I can understand why parents embrace the labels of "indigo" and "crystal" children. Tyler even identified with the label at one point in his life and was interviewed on one of

Boston's main news networks about being an "indigo" child.

Paradoxically the attributes associated with the "indigo" child label contributed to Tyler's depression as well as his healing. Tyler can sense people's emotions just by being in their presence. He could become easily overwhelmed with all these emotions at the mall or other crowded places. It was the negative emotions he was feeling from others that affected him the most and contributed to his depression and cutting himself. Because of the "indigo" child identification, I sent him to a spiritual counselor who worked with "indigo" children rather than a more traditional counselor. I knew this spiritual counselor would see Tyler as a whole person of spirit going through a spiritual crisis rather than broken and needing to be fixed. Tyler needed help in understanding the darkness surrounding him in order to reconnect with his sacred unified self. We did not medicate because drugs felt like a symbolic negation of what Tyler was experiencing as his "dark night of the soul." I trusted the Unified spirit to guide us and he did emerge with a much deeper understanding of his sacred purpose in life.

I do believe there are children who come into this physical world more spiritually aware. In other words, they remember more clearly their spiritual essence. And I also believe these children are often the ones we label with a disability or disorder because they think and perceive the world differently from culturally sanctioned ways. Sometimes this can lead to intense unhappiness as they cannot figure out how to reconcile what they know intuitively with what society is telling them. If the ego begins to override their spiritual, unified self then it can lead to disconnection with the truth of who they are and lead to what we call the mental disorders such as depression, bipolar disorder, or schizophrenia. Many of these children are also the ones we label as having attention deficit disorder or learning disabilities.

William Stillman writes lovingly in his books about the spiritual awareness and connectedness of children within the autism spectrum. Many of these children are also thought to be "indigo" and "crystal" children. Martha Beck in *Expecting Adam* describes the gentleness and spiritual wisdom of her son Adam, with Down syndrome. Many of our children with special needs labels do not fit within the "indigo" or "crystal" child definition but possess spiritual knowingness. Another example of this is Mattie Stepanek, a boy with muscular dystrophy who wrote wonderful spiritual poems about life called *Heartsongs*.

The Unified Spirit may lead us to believe our children with disabilities or disorders are more spiritually aware. This may help us drop the self-limiting beliefs that lead us to view our children as defective, as implied by their more traditional labels. However, the "indigo" and "crystal" children labels are still labels with expectations of behavior that can limit our perceptions of our child. Seeing past the labels to the spirit within the child is a step toward remembering we are all spiritual beings and thus extensions of God's love.

Remember, it is not about fixing or saving the world, it is about changing our minds about the world; removing the blocks to love's awareness. Perhaps these children provide more of an opportunity to experience the mystical and thus open our hearts to the possibility that we are more than these physical bodies. In this sense, these children do help us to realize the truth of who we are. They can be a bridge to greater understanding when we can accept the possibility that there is much more to life than the ego-driven traditional, scientific, medical model view of the world. Tyler certainly provided this possibility to me.

Seeing Past the Labels

Seeing past the labels or the behavior to the whole child is one of the first steps on our journey to spiritual parenting. One way to do this is to think about what happens when we give power to a label. Imagine you have a sign attached to your chest that lists all of your strengths and gifts. Imagine what type of conversations you would have with your friends, family, and strangers. They will probably respond positively to what they see on your sign and they will think you can take care of yourself. Now imagine you have a sign attached to your chest that lists all of your problems and deficits. Now imagine the type of conversations you would have with your family, friends, and strangers. When you want to talk about the positive or your accomplishments, all they see are the deficits listed on your sign and they respond accordingly and then will probably try to fix you.

The children we label walk around as if they have a huge sign plastered to their chest labeling all of their deficits and we expect them to act according to their sign. We assume behavior based on the list of deficits. And it is no wonder some of our labeled children are angry, anxious, and depressed. Labels can become self-fulfilling prophecies.

Labels are for products not children. Labels box our children into a list of expectations based on the implied deficits. When children want to act outside of the box of expectations, they are often forced back into the box because their actions do not make sense within the label's definition. This is true whether it is for the special needs label, for labels implying normality, or for the more positive spiritual or gifted labels.

We can embrace this idea that children are not their labels, yet we often feel the need for the diagnosis or label in order to secure needed services for our child. We often use the label because we want others to understand the difficulties we are experiencing. Or we use the more positive labels to bolster our self worth. Sometimes we want people to see us as long suffering parents who have more than their share to deal with. I used the label of learning disability to make sure Tyler received the appropriate education he needed. He still has to use the label to explain himself to teachers in college or to get the accommodations he needs to cope and succeed.

How can we play this cultural game without allowing the

labels to define who our children are? Once again it is about detaching ourselves from believing the label, realizing it does not define our child. We give power to the label by creating a story around it, making it real with our emotions of anger, sadness, and worry, which are all about fear of the future for our child. One way to begin to release the power of a label is to change the story into a positive story and then it becomes easier to release the label as having any power to affect our happiness.

One way to begin to change the story in order to remember the truth of your child is to write a poem about your child's spirit. I developed this activity for one of my parenting workshops. The poem is modeled after Sara Moores Campbell's poem, *Give Us the Spirit of the Child.*[6] Anyone can write a poem using the structure I provide. Usually there are few parents who say they write creatively but they soon change their mind once they start writing. This is always the favorite activity of the parents in my workshop. It helps parents focus on the essence of their child, not the label. Many of the parents share the poem with their child, which can open avenues of communication because the poem says, I see you, I see the truth of you. (Please see appendix for the directions and structure on writing a poem about your child.)

To test the structure of writing a poem, I used it to write a poem about Tyler. I offer it not as an example of a great poem but as an example of how it helped to see past Tyler's labels to what I thought was his spiritual self. I wrote this poem when Tyler was around 10 years old. As I read it now, I am struck by how much it still describes Tyler. When we allow ourselves to think out of the box of our traditional perceptions, then we begin to see the eternal essence of our child.

Give me the spirit of Tyler
A spirit like a flame, orange and red with
Flashing moments of bright white and
Blazing blue

Give me Tyler's spirit like the gazelle
Graceful, gentle but alert and quick to run
Becoming like the mother tiger fierce and loyal.

Give me Tyler's spirit, flowing circle,
Always changing, always moving, always inclusive.

Give me Tyler's spirit connecting us all
Through imagination and uniqueness

Give me Tyler's spirit that says "see me beautiful."

The reality is we are one in spirit. However, while we are in these physical bodies we are all different in myriad ways. Being able to honor these differences is paradoxically a path to remembering we are all one. Culturally we decide that some differences are less acceptable than others and we try to fix those differences in an effort to make everyone the same or more like us.

Judith Snow, a woman with severe physical limitations, can only use her thumb. However, she travels the world speaking about her vision of an inclusive community. She writes and talks about how every person has two gifts, presence and difference. We are all here as human beings and we are all different from each other in countless ways. Therefore, walking or not walking, hearing or being deaf, quiet and contained or highly energetic, behaving as expected or disturbing others, seeing or not seeing—all are gifts arising from difference. These differences add to the diversity of the human community and offer opportunities for meaningful interaction and spiritual connection.[7] The ego wants us to believe that some differences are worse than others. When we can see differences as opportunities to connect with another, it is a first step toward seeing past the label or behavior to the divine light within. We begin to realize we are all one spirit as an extension of God's love.

I found Thomas Armstrong during a time in my journey when I was searching for professionals who viewed children in alternative and affirming ways. His book, *Radiant Child,* opened up a whole new path of exploration of seeing the divine spirit in every child. The following quote expresses the idea of appreciating the spiritual essence of our children. It is through the unconditional love we have for our children that many of us can begin the journey to unconditional love for everyone. If we can see the radiance in our children then we can believe all of us have that radiance inside. If we embrace the opportunity our children provide for exploration of self then they can truly be a bridge to understanding and forgiving this physical world.

> *This is the essence of the radiant child. Belonging to both heaven and earth, the radiant child dances into our lives as a bridge between dark and light, body and spirit, ego and self, the individual and God. The radiant child spans and sings this wholeness in every fiber. We would all be wise to listen. Even better to sing and dance along!* [8]

Another way to see past the label to the whole child is to reframe the negative words and descriptions used about your child. I first came across the idea of reframing the descriptions about our children from another Thomas Armstrong book, The *Myth of the ADD Child, Fifty Ways to Improve Your Child's Behavior and Attention Span without Drugs, Labels, or Coercion.* Before exploring how to reframe negative descriptions, it is helpful to understand the stories we create about our child and why we create these stories.

We make up stories about our children all the time based on what we want for our child and based on the perceptions of others. And in so doing, we often make assumptions about why our children behave a certain way. Eventually we will explore how to love what is without creating a story, but right now as we begin our journey it is helpful to understand that we create stories about our children with our thoughts and beliefs.

We often buy into the current belief system about our child's label and then we create a story using that belief system. It is invariably a negative story. One of the ways to get us out of this negative story is to reframe the negative words being used into positive words. We are still creating a story based on assumptions, but a positive story will provide a bridge to eventually seeing our child's wholeness and realizing that no child is a mistake. The following quote from Armstrong's *Myth of the ADD Child*, gives an example of reframing the common negative descriptions used to describe children with the label of Attention Deficit Disorder.[9]

Instead of thinking of the ADD child as..........	Think of him or her as...............
hyperactive	*energetic*
impulsive	*spontaneous*
distractible	*creative*
a daydreamer	*imaginative*
inattentive	*global thinker with a wide focus*
unpredictable	*flexible*
argumentative	*independent*
stubborn	*committed*
irritable	*sensitive*
aggressive	*assertive*
attention deficit disordered	*unique*

In my workshops I have participants think of all the negative words used to describe children with special needs labels and then we try and think of more positive words to use. I invite you to do the same with the negative words used by professionals and perhaps yourself about your child. I guarantee that if you can own the new positive story, your child will feel your positive energy and will respond accordingly. It is just a small step to rising above the label and only responding to the light and truth of your child.

Another tool I use to focus on the spirit within my child is the Buddhist "Loving Kindness" meditation. The idea behind the meditation is to focus thoughts of loving kindness on ourselves, the people close to us, and the people we have problems with. There are several variations; however, most use a combination of the following. May (I or name) be safe. May (I or Name) be peaceful. May (I or name) be happy. You can add your own words. Take some deep breaths to still your thoughts and visualize your child or someone who upsets you, then repeat the words as a chant or to yourself. Karen Drucker has put the meditation to music and for me singing the words releases judgments and brings me immediately back to peace. After singing loving kindness for yourself, substitute your child's name for the word "I."

Here are her words.

Loving Kindness

May I be filled with loving kindness
May I be well
May I be peaceful and at ease
And may I be happy[10]

Once I am back in peace and have released the incessant fearful and judging thoughts, I feel blessed and the voice of the Unified Spirit can be heard. Once again we can surrender to the spiritual current within and accept what is. We know within the depth of our being, no child is a mistake; that our child is perfect in God's eyes, that we are all perfect in God's eyes.

Chapter III

The Gift of a Question

You are either attaching to your thoughts or inquiring. There is no other choice.
–Byron Katie, *Loving What Is*

Seeing past the label and holding the wholeness of our child are first steps to parenting from a place of peace. Every day Tyler would, and still does, gift me with his spiritual insights, his artistic creations, and his kindness toward others. It was easy to see Tyler as much more than his label implied. However, I was stuck blaming everyone else for seeing our children as defective, especially the educational and medical communities. I fell into the trap of believing I was right and everyone else was wrong. I had so much angry energy around this subject that I was making myself unhappy and definitely not changing anyone else's mind. It took a lot of internal inquiry before I understood the dynamics of attaching feelings to my thoughts of having to always be right about my beliefs and how this did not help to parent from a place of peace.

As parents of children with special needs labels we can also easily get hooked into thinking we have to totally protect our children from a world that does not appreciate them. And, we often find ourselves on a spiritual path to try and understand why these children are in our lives. Many of us have some understanding that healing comes from within ourselves. As we become more spiritually aware we begin to think we have all the answers or at least knowledge of the many paths and methods for spiritual healing. Sometimes we use this knowledge, with all good intentions, to help the people in our lives, specifically our partner or child with a label or any struggling child. Feeling we know best often becomes a subtle attempt to control.

We rebel against those who view our children as defective and needing to be fixed. We need to be careful that our own spiritual attempts to help our children do not fall also into the category of "fixing" them. We forget our children have their own path to follow. We cannot control their behavior, we can only guide. There is a subtle difference between efforts to convince our children of our wisdom and providing guidance. We want to short circuit our children's struggles, because after all, they are already struggling enough. However when we do this, we deny their own life's path, their own lessons, their own spiritual memories.

Backing off and allowing our children to experience their own lessons can seem like an impossible task if our child is engaging in what we perceive as self-destructive behavior. The more we push, the more the child pushes back or stays rigid in his or her path. One of the most difficult lessons for a parent is to let go in the face of self-destructive behavior. I am not implying that certain behavior is not tolerated if it is hurtful and, there are consequences to behavior. We can still state our opinions and model our beliefs. But we cannot force a child to share our spiritual wisdom or learn our lessons. Constantly saying, "I know best," "This is what you should do," will only result in resistance. State your case and beliefs and then let it go and give it over to the Unified Spirit. The Unified Spirit works in every one of us, including our children.

The most reasonable and immediate response to Tyler cutting himself was to throw out his razor blades and tell him to not buy any more. Ultimately this did not work as he secretly found ways to buy more. He had to look within to understand his need to cut. I could not force this awareness on him. So I gave it over to the Unified Spirit which led me to an appropriate spiritual counselor for Tyler. While giving guidance and support, I demonstrated to

Tyler my unshakable love and faith that he had the spiritual wisdom within to heal himself.

We cannot even begin to know the spiritual plan for our children. We do not know what lessons of forgiveness are there for them. We have to do a lot to forgive those who see our children as broken and in need of fixing. And our children have a lot to forgive in those who want to fix them. As we heal ourselves we heal the whole, including our children. It does not come from insisting they adopt our own moral and spiritual beliefs. It comes from our own forgiveness and healing.

You cannot change your child; you cannot change the system's attitude to your child; you can only change your mind about your child. Remember your relationship with your child is holy ground and holy ground is risky ground. It can feel scary to look within and confront our fears and drop judgments to embrace the divine in each of us.

When you are in that place of feeling stuck or upset with your child, give yourself the gift of a question. We rarely take the time to ask our child what is wrong, we make assumptions instead. And often our assumptions are not at all what our child perceives is the difficulty. The question can lead to hearing our children's story. In our busy, fast-paced lives we often do not take the time to listen to our children's stories. We need to learn to listen from a place of total presence, not thinking about what still needs to be done in our day such as what groceries to buy, just be present with our child. We listen from that place of stillness when the Unified Spirit is in charge. We listen without judging, without forcing our own interpretation, just accepting whatever our child is telling us. When we can listen from a place of unconditional love, then the healing begins.

When Tyler was in kindergarten, he insisted on fantasy dressing every morning before going to school. He wanted to be a ninja turtle, a power ranger, or superman to name just a few of his fantasy characters. I allowed myself to go slightly crazy each morning arguing with him to dress in normal clothes and then finally giving in. I just thought he was being overly creative. I was always on a tight schedule trying to make breakfast, get two children off to school, exercise, meditate, get dressed and make the train in time to go into Boston for my full-time job. I did not take the time to listen to what Tyler was telling me by wanting to dress up as a fantasy figure every morning.

One afternoon when Tyler and I were alone together, I asked him why he could not dress as Tyler to go to school. He answered that he could not be Tyler and he started to cry. This one question and my willingness to listen allowed me to see life through Tyler's eyes. It was a wake-up call, a confirmation from those niggling thoughts in the back of my head that something was not quite right. I now understood his dressing as a fantasy figure was a creative coping strategy. I became his ally instead of constantly fighting him in the morning. We chose what he would wear the night before. Then my creative side also was engaged. We talked about his interests, which were fish and dinosaurs. He then created a wonderful dinosaur and a fish out of wood. These props allowed him to dress in normal clothes while being a paleontologist or an oceanographer. It had the unintended benefit of the teacher and children seeing his artistic gifts rather than focusing solely on what he could not do.

It is amazing what a question followed by unconditional listening will do for a struggling child, an adult, and yourself. The lesson of not making assumptions about my children's behavior or other people's behavior is something I have to learn over and over again. I can still get caught in an argument with my children or my spouse and then realize I am making assumptions about behavior, judging, and not listening.

Over the years I gained an awareness that I needed to change, not my children or spouse. However, most of us cannot just say to ourselves, I will think differently, I will act differently, I will not take on my child's pain, I will not judge, I will not be angry.

We need the tools to examine our beliefs before we can let them go. I would tell myself over and over again to let go of an angry thought or a hurt with little success. Instead, I buried the anger or the hurt, thinking I had let it go. And then the hurt feeling or anger would erupt later when least expected.

Carl Jung called this place where we bury all our unwanted thoughts, feelings, hurts, shame, and anger "the shadow." He taught we needed to explore our shadow and bring it to the light in order to heal ourselves. Having the courage to inquire within and look at all those things we abhor about ourselves is part of our spiritual journey. And when we do, we find they are nothing but thoughts, they are not the truth of who we are.

The Shame and Blame Game

One of the most damaging of emotions is shame. If we feel ashamed of our children because of their behavior or their label, then we feel ashamed of ourselves. This feeling was expressed over and over again by parents in my workshops or in individual consultation. We care about what people think because we feel they are judging us as bad or incompetent parents. How could you have allowed your stepson to rape your daughter? How come your child has uncontrollable tantrums in public? How come your son cuts himself? How come your daughter is insolent and oppositional? How could you possibly allow your child to become so depressed he or she became suicidal?

All the various disorders and disabilities are associated with shame; however, alcoholism, drug addiction, obsessive compulsive disorder, bipolar disorder, schizophrenia, and autism seem to be more susceptible to immense family shame. There seems to be a lot of social judgment associated with disorders and disabilities—some more than others. And it is the judgment of others that we fear and we judge ourselves the most. It becomes a viscous circle.

When Tyler was depressed and cutting, I had done the work

of inquiry so I was able to parent from a place of calm and trust. Yet, after he emerged from his depression and I received his ok to talk about it, I found myself sliding into feeling shame. I wanted to mention the experience in my workshops, but I had a momentary fear of people judging me for being a bad mother. Yet when I opened up about the experience, I found other parents who were experiencing similar situations and were relieved to have someone talk about it. When I let go of my shame, others let go of theirs.

Tyler continues to offer challenges to me about shame. He is slowly tattooing most of his body, plus he has gauges in his ears which create very large holes for rings or discs. They are jarring and one of the first things people notice about Tyler. He sees his body as a canvas for his art. There have been moments in public when I felt uncomfortable with the way people looked at Tyler. I fear they are judging me for allowing my son to look the way he is.

Tyler says one of his life's missions is to demonstrate the misconceptions that occur when judging someone by appearance. A noble idea, I say to myself, but why does he have to pick such a startling way of doing it? Why add such a different appearance to his list of struggles? So this shame, it can creep up on you unexpectedly. I have to be vigilant and continue to examine my thoughts and beliefs, which lead to judgment. The tattoos do not bother me anymore. In fact, I have come to like them and what they represent about Tyler's life. What is important is my son is a spiritually centered, kind, and compassionate human being.

Yet for all my work, the gauges in the ears still bother me. So I continually give myself the gift of a question. It is like peeling an onion. Every time I question my beliefs and thoughts, I peel more of the onion away until eventually I get at the core belief causing the unhappiness and I can let it drop.

Shame is closely associated with blame. We need to blame someone or something for our child's difficulties. We blame others and the professionals blame us. We want to say, look, it is not my fault, it is my child's brain, or my child hangs out with the wrong set of kids, or he is allergic to something that triggered the bizarre behavior, or it is the vaccine, or she was born with addictive behavior, or he inherited the tendency to emotional instability. We want to be able to say to people, look, I am innocent, I did not cause this, and someone or something else did. I am not to blame. Or, we make it worse by blaming ourselves, which prevents us from seeing our child's wholeness of spirit.

I participated in a workshop with a woman who was in much pain and sorrow because her daughter struggled with learning difficulties. She believed it was her fault caused by the drugs she took while pregnant. She questioned how to let go of this belief, stuck with the conviction that it was true and therefore she should suffer. So tenacious was she in holding onto this belief, she could not see that her unhappiness about a past event that could not be changed was keeping her from having a loving, present relationship with her daughter. Not only was she giving her power to a label, she was giving her power to obsessing about a past event. This belief that she should suffer meant she could not see the beauty in her child, all she saw was the struggles. Sometimes the most difficult person to forgive is oneself.

When we accept society's labels for our children, we seek to place our blame outside us. Or we accept responsibility but turn our blame inward and judge ourselves. If I am going to get stuck this is where I do, judging myself, not forgiving myself. And when this happens, I know I have totally succumbed to the ego's thought system of guilt and attack. When I am in this dark place, it feels even more difficult to get out. And the ego is really clever, because I will tell myself I know better, look at all the spiritual work I have done, how could I possibly be this unforgiving? How do we get out of the shame and blame game? How do we get out of the ego's grip? You give yourself the gift of a question.

Removing the Blocks to Love's Awareness

Another way of looking at this is to realize that our essence is love. In this spiritual classroom our job is to remove the obstacles to love's awareness, that which we already are.[11] We do not search for love, peace, or enlightenment; we already are love and peace, the light of God. However, as physical beings we have accumulated thoughts and beliefs that block our remembrance of who we truly are. I love this following quote from the poet Rumi, "Your task is not to seek for love, but merely to seek and find all the barriers within yourself that you have built against it."

Barry (Bears) Neil Kaufman with the "Option Process® Dialogue" and Byron Katie with "The Work" are two excellent resources for helping us remove the blocks to love's awareness. They have both developed questions we can use to understand our beliefs, which are just thoughts with feelings attached. The Option Process® Dialogue is what I used first for my inquiry work. Then I discovered Byron Katie and found her four simple questions comprising The Work often helped when I was not making any progress with the Option Process® Dialogue. I now use both methods. When one set of questions does not work, then I try the other set of questions. I have even developed my own set of questions. Fear can be tenacious in its grip to keep you unhappy and blaming others, so I will use whatever tool works at the time to bring me back to a place of peace. (Please see the resources section for more information about the Option Process® Dialogue and The Work.)

It was while I was researching information about alternative programs for different disabilities for my first book, that I discovered the Option Institute in western Massachusetts. Not only did I learn about a wonderful program for children within the autism spectrum, I found a place for my own spiritual growth. The program for children is called the Son-Rise

Program® of the Autism Treatment Center of America. The description on the website captured my attention and I immediately wanted to visit. "This unique treatment program, based on an attitude of love and acceptance, is profoundly gentle, non-judgmental and respectful of the child's world and creates maximum opportunity for growth."[12]

In order to visit the Son-Rise Program® I took a week-long workshop at the Option Institute, which then led to taking their eight-week course called "Living the Dream." This was a life-changing experience which, to this day, continues to provide the ideas and tools I use to question any upsetting event in order to discover the beliefs that take me out of joy. For eight weeks I deconstructed my ego. I bounced between fear and love. The fear showed itself primarily as anger, shame, defensiveness, and sadness. Much of my work focused on my sadness about Tyler's struggles.

This is where I learned the gift of a question. My interpretation of the basic teachings of the Option Institute has provided an enduring structure for understanding the lessons in my spiritual classroom, which I share with you here. All of us have beliefs that are created from thoughts resulting from our life experiences. All actions are the result of the following formula: stimulus-belief-response. Some neutral event (stimulus) instantaneously triggers a belief and then we respond accordingly. Every event is neutral until we attach a belief to it.

In one of my workshops for parents, a single mother who had adopted a girl was upset because her daughter would eat almost nothing except macaroni and cheese. She had a belief that if her daughter did not eat a balanced, healthy meal, she was a bad mother. Eating macaroni and cheese was a neutral stimulus that triggered the belief, "I'm a bad mother," which led to the response of constant worry and fighting to get her daughter to eat something else.

Assume nothing about another person's actions because we

cannot truly understand another person's thoughts or reasons for behaving a certain way. We can probably guess at some of the assumptions the mother was making in this macaroni and cheese scenario. One obvious assumption she expressed was that her daughter would be permanently harmed by eating macaroni and cheese and that she might do this for the rest of her life. Another Option teaching comes into play in this scenario, there is no right, wrong, good or bad and each one of us is our own best expert. The mother was unsure of herself, she did not trust in her own wisdom nor did she trust in her daughter's wisdom. She thought just eating macaroni and cheese was bad and that there was a right way to eat. She was unaware that both she and her daughter were doing the best they could with the information they both had at the time.

The gift of a question not only for herself but also for her daughter could allow the examination of the beliefs she held about what makes a good mother. She is not a bad mother just because her daughter only eats macaroni and cheese. That is just a detail pointing to a larger belief. Beliefs lie in the details. I could not just tell her it was ok and her daughter would be all right. She had to gain this awareness herself. She had to do her own internal work. She is her own best expert. She has the divine wisdom inside herself.

One mother I was working with was upset by her son's disrespectful attitude toward her. It manifested in his leaving yogurt containers on the coffee table no matter how many times his mother asked him not to. I suggested she ask him without anger why he left the yogurt container on the table. To her surprise, he was not trying to defy her and he was surprised his mother felt he was being disrespectful. He knew she was mad but, he had no idea why. To him, a yogurt container on the coffee table was insignificant.

We often assume a reason for people's behavior that may or may not be what the person is intending but our assumption makes us unhappy. A simple event such as leaving a yogurt container can get blown out of proportion to the actual event, based on an assumption. Instead of assuming, first ask a question that will help you see the world through your child's eyes.

These are just two small examples of what all of us do at times — create mountains out of mole hills based on assumptions. We allow our egoic thoughts to create scenarios about events and consequences that may or may not happen. This can become even more acute with our children who struggle, because their problems seem bigger. But in reality, it is all the same. Each event is neutral. It is our thoughts based on our beliefs that cause us to react.

There are no neutral thoughts because they are always based on judgment of past events or knowledge. Whatever you say or do cannot make me angry or upset. I have a choice to be angry or upset. Ask yourself why one event can cause someone to become angry and the same event gets no reaction from someone else. It is our thoughts based on a belief that determines whether or not we will be upset or angry, not the event itself. One way to begin to understand this concept is through the Option Institute's teaching of stimulus-belief-response, which also leads to understanding that there are no right, wrong, good, or bad thoughts or events.

Tyler and Sarah ate a lot of macaroni and cheese. I was just grateful they would eat and I thought macaroni and cheese was healthy for a growing child. This did not upset me because it did not push my "I am a bad mother" button. Other things did, like letting Tyler watch TV.

Tyler learns visually, not by reading. I could get into a bad place about this quickly because it pushed my bad mother button. How many parents have I listened to and how many articles have I read about how harmful TV is for our children? I counteracted some of this by trying to have Tyler watch only educational or uplifting videos of my choice. It was a fight I soon gave up and trusted Tyler to pick what he wanted. He would pick shows that made him laugh. Sometimes, he just wanted the background noise while he created something amazing out of whatever material he could find. He was constantly pestering me for materials for his creations. He would go searching in his father's work room for all kinds of building material. He demonstrated it was possible to make anything out of duct and electrical tape. Once after watching the movie "Titanic," he created a boat out of all the Kleenex boxes in the house and legos. (I ended up with a lot of Kleenex.) Watching TV definitely did not ruin him.

This is not to start a debate about the pros and cons of watching TV. It is to point out that there are no right, wrong, good, or bad decisions or events. When anything upsets us or pushes our buttons, it is time to go inward and ask our questions to discover the belief that is driving our unhappiness. Then the Unified Spirit can guide us to do what is best for our child. It is something inside of us that needs to be questioned. We choose to be angry, upset, afraid, worried; no one makes us feel these emotions. We all have the wisdom inside, the still, small voice within. Through inquiry we access the wisdom that tells us to let go of the core beliefs that make us unhappy.

We can re-write our story about our children from one of sadness and struggle to one of joy and peace, but first we have to look at the beliefs that cause us to stay stuck in the sadness and struggle. Most people have difficulty just saying to themselves, "I will be happy," and then feeling happy. While coping with our child's struggles, it helps to first look at the small stuff before tackling the larger problems in our close relationship with our child. If you are experiencing any type of resistance to peace in any circumstance, however, it can feel huge to you and small to an outside observer.

An example of this for me is my relationship to spring in New England. I grew up in Texas and Oklahoma where spring is warm and starts in March or April. In New England spring is noted for being wet and cool. Every spring I would complain about the cool weather and the endless days of rain interspersed with a few sunny, warm days. I appreciated the beautiful flowers but bemoaned the seemingly endless days of wet and cool weather. Every year my New England friends would remark that the spring was cooler and more rainy than usual. This response always makes me want to slap my head in amazement; they never seem to remember that last spring was just as rainy and cool. I finally decided New Englanders have a kind of selective amnesia that is necessary for them to survive the long, hard winters and cool wet springtimes.

I have a friend who loves the misty, drizzly, cloudy, cool days of New England spring. I thought she was delusional and would not feel that way if she had ever experienced a truly warm and lovely spring. She moved to southern California, the land of perpetual sunshine. Now she wishes for more rain and cool days and I wish for more warmth and sunny days. I cannot help but feel we are both where we need to be in our spiritual classroom, learning to be happy wherever we are despite the weather.

I began to realize I was making myself miserable and annoying everyone around me over something I could not control. When I am totally stuck in the ego, I become angry because I feel I have no control. So I did a lot of inquiry work to release and be ok with cool, wet weather in New England lasting until June. It has been a slow process of first, not complaining about the cool weather, and second, finding ways to enjoy the sun when it does arrive and just appreciate the moment. So I just changed my expectations for warmth and less rain to occur mid-June and it has worked for the past few years, until this year.

As I am writing, our spring and summer, even for New England, has been unusually cloudy, cool, and rainy and uh oh, it is now July and there appears to be no end in sight for the cool rainy days. My story of not expecting it to get sunny until June, which allowed me to stay calm, just came crashing down. Here I am once again letting the weather bother me, so it is back to the basics. Clearly I am still learning to love whatever happens. I need to dig deeper with my questions. And this is what happens with our children who are struggling, it is a process. We reach a plateau of some peace and contentment and then something happens to jar our calmness and we find we have to dig deeper with our questions to keep discovering the beliefs that are keeping us unhappy.

I think the selective amnesia New Englanders have about spring helps them cope and be hopeful and look forward to the next spring. They only remember the sun and the flowers, while I only remember the cloudy days and the rain. So while the facts support that New England springs are rainy and cool, true New Englanders have created a story that allows them to look forward to spring and appreciate the few days of warmth and the beautiful flowers without complaining about the rain. I can do the same thing, but I cannot do it without finding out first why it makes me so unhappy. Until I thoroughly understand why I think I need warm springs and summers to be happy, any story I create that helps me cope will eventually fail to work.

Creating a more positive story is just one step in the process of learning how to be at peace without needing a story, just accepting what is. There is a difference between needing and wanting. I can want warmth and sunshine, but when my want becomes a need then it becomes a script for unhappiness, because weather will never always be warm and sunny. So if I need warmth to be happy, then there will be a considerable amount of time in my life when I will be unhappy. Why should I give away my power to be at peace to something I cannot control?

The same occurs with our children. We can want our children not to have to struggle, not to experience any pain or unhappiness, not to have a disability or disorder but, when we decide we need them to be "normal" or not to have to struggle in order for us to be happy, then we will be unhappy, because our children will experience loss, pain, and struggle as a part of life. We can continually do our inquiry work, gradually release unhelpful beliefs, and create a story that allows us to be happy with our children. And creating a happy story brings us closer to being able to accept what is, and whatever shows up in our lives. And when we can accept what is without its having any power to affect us, then that is true joy and peace.

A wonderful learning about dropping a core belief happened in relation to an event again involving Tyler. When he was fourteen, he was a counselor in training (CIT) for our town's community summer camp run by the recreation department. He enjoyed the experience of working with the littlest kids as it was an extension of his positive experience of being a teen aide for the little ones at our church. The children seemed to love him.

The following summer we thought he would automatically be asked to be a CIT again. Then we heard that his friends had been asked but not Tyler. Thinking it was just an oversight, I called the camp director. They agreed to interview Tyler and reconsider if he wanted the job so much. That night they called and told me they did not think Tyler could keep up and they appreciated his learning difference but their first loyalty was to the other children. I was enraged, their reasoning felt bogus. I cried, I ranted and raved at people who did not understand. I had created a need for Tyler to always have a summer job without having to struggle each summer to find one. When that fell through, I was unhappy. All the time I had spent at the Option Insitute, letting go of self-limiting beliefs, not making wants into needs, and my sadness about Tyler's struggles, seemed to vanish in an instant. At some point in my wallowing in unhappiness, I realized Tyler was just fine. He had accepted what had happened and had moved on. I was the one who was still stuck and making myself miserable. I finally remembered to ask myself a question and then I started dialoguing as I was taught to do at the Option

Institute.

It took several days of off-and-on inquiry work to finally realize the core belief that was keeping me unhappy. I realized I thought I could not change people's treatment of Tyler and children with labels unless they saw the pain, the struggle, and the sadness. I immediately thought, "This is not how I want people to see Tyler or any child with a special-needs label. I want to show their beauty, their strengths, and their gifts. I want people to see the radiance that is Tyler and all children." And with this awareness, I was able to permanently drop the belief causing me to rant and rave and cry about others' perceptions of Tyler.

I learned that the gift of a question works not only with the small stuff but with the larger, more painful events. I spent a lot of time doing internal work when Tyler was so depressed and was banging on walls until his fists bled, and then cutting himself. Tyler's cutting also happened at a time when my husband and I were in couple therapy to save our marriage. And then my father died. Even though periodically I would allow myself to get caught in the pain, at the same time I knew I was walking with the Goddess, which, at the time, was my symbol of the Unified Spirit. Often, I felt as if part of me was detached and observing the events in my life.

Eckhart Tollé, with his teaching about living in the present, talks about how just observing what you are doing can have a powerful effect on living in the now. Too often we go about our lives mindlessly, just reacting to life's events. We obsess about the past and worry about the future. As parents, we obsess about our child's diagnosis or struggles and then worry about how it will affect our child's future. We cannot change the past and we have no idea what the future will bring. We do not need to obsess or worry in order to parent our child. When we do this we miss the peace of the eternal moment. In the eternal moment, our child is safe and loved and all we need to know about parenting is there.

Byron Katie's four questions that comprise The Work, are a wonderful way to examine the thoughts that take us out of peace and keep us from living in the present moment.[13] Through her questions, I have been able to understand that the thoughts I create about a person or an event are what cause a life of stress. One of my most powerful insights from doing The Work, is realizing that in each moment I am safe and at peace.

Ask yourself the next time you feel stressed or upset what you are feeling in just one brief moment without any thoughts. In the stillness of that fleeting moment you are safe, you are well, you are loved, and you are peace. Our spiritual journey is to learn to extend the fleeting moment to encompass our entire life. I have found the only way to do this is to give myself the gift of a question, whether it is from the Option Process® Dialogue, The Work., or my own questions. Changing our mind to see with the eyes of the Unified Spirit is the miracle that undoes the past in the present, and releases the future.

Both The Work and the Option Process® Dialogue can also be used with and by children to help them examine the beliefs which keep them unhappy and struggling. While similar in principle, I find Dr Ross Greene's Collaborative Problem Solving (CPS) approach to be the most useful when working with children and modeling for them ways they can access their inner guide. Even though Dr Greene is a psychiatrist, he sees the diagnostic labels we give our children – especially those with behavioral, emotional and social challenges – as ineffective in helping these children learn to get along in the world. I find his approach immensely compassionate and very effective.

Using Collaborative Problem Solving with children provides a way to see the world through the child's eyes, to understand their perspective and then collaboratively work toward solutions that are mutually satisfactory. While Dr Greene is committed to working with children who adults consider difficult and opposi-tional, his approach works with all relationships. At his website, www.livesinthebalance.org Dr Greene provides free resources and videos to take someone step by step through the process. I recommend all parents visit this website even if your child does not have a special needs label.

My experience of peace grows each day as I more readily remember to use the tools to examine my beliefs and listen to the voice of the Unified Spirit rather than the ego. Yet, I am still learning to live all of my life in complete peace, free of worried thoughts. I understand that my past is over and does not have any power to affect me. And I am beginning to understand the teaching that any thought that creates worry about the future is a thought about the past.

At times I still worry about the future, about having enough money, about my children's ability to cope, about my husband's ability to be at peace, about the weather. And my worry about the future is based on what I believe has happened in the past. I still allow some people to upset or irritate me. Sometimes, I still react to what is going on in the world. Sometimes I allow myself to become unhappy with the weather. As a result, I continually give myself the gift of a question and each time I do, a small chink is removed in the wall I built to keep me from remembering the truth of who I am.

Chapter IV

We Are Always Doing the Best We Can

Is having a child with a disability a curse or a blessing? A cross or an anchor? A barrier to what I really want to do, or a lightening rod for my priorities? At different times it is probably each of these things, but our attitude can tip the balance, one way or the other, so that most of the time it is an anchor and a blessing—or a curse and a cross—depending on how we have chosen to approach it. So many people search endlessly for 'meaning' in their lives, often resisting the meaning that is right there. The point is not that we are lucky to have a child with a disability because it gives our lives instant meaning. The point is that to be presented with this event, and to fail to engage it as an opportunity—for focus, for meaning, for learning and growth, for a way to affect the world we live in—is to miss the experience that life has offered us. However, as Arnold Beisser points out in *Flying Without Wings*, "In order to see the opportunities, though, you must accept what happened as if you have chosen it."
–Barbara Gill, *Changed by a Child*

Woven throughout the chapters in this book is the idea that we can choose how to see our situation with a labeled child. I have talked about doing inquiry work to uncover the beliefs that keep us unhappy about our child. I have also talked about some techniques that help us see past the labels to the divine light in our children. When we accept the idea of embracing our experience with a labeled child for learning and growth, it means we accept that we are in a spiritual classroom.

Choosing to engage as an opportunity the event of having a

child with a disability or disorder, does not come easily for some parents. I have been in parent groups in which most parents resented having to parent a child with a disability or disorder, and some were bitter. They felt life had dealt them a bad hand. Suggesting they could change their minds to be at peace was met with, "You cannot possibly understand the situation I am in." No one can be talked into seeing their situation differently. However, I can give the same understanding I would give to children with labels. I can meet people where they are, recognizing that their fear is also my fear. I can either judge people and myself for being stuck or realize that we are all doing the best we can with the information and awareness we have in the moment. And if you feel yourself in this place of resentment, you can also realize that you are doing the best you can.

I have written about how our beliefs shape our response to life events. It is helpful to review this once again. All of us hold beliefs (thoughts with emotions attached) that feel sacrosanct, so when someone questions these beliefs, we often take it personally and become upset. In other words, we decide certain beliefs define who we are and therefore are the truth. If someone believes differently from me, then they are wrong because my beliefs are the truth. Even if I am attacked, questioning my beliefs is too scary because I have decided my beliefs define who I am; therefore I defend and attack instead. This is a prescription for all arguments that can escalate into wars. The social psychologists call this cognitive dissonance.

Cognitive dissonance occurs when we behave in ways that contradict a deeply held attitude. When people experience cognitive dissonance, it is especially unpleasant and they will feel strongly motivated to resolve it in order to feel comfortable again. Since we cannot change past behavior, people will justify their behavior by reinforcing the deeply held attitude that they feel is an essential part of who they are. Parents verbally hurt their child, however they believe they are good parents therefore they decide their child's behavior caused them to be hurtful or, that the verbal abuse was necessary to toughen up their child to survive in this world. A wonderful book to read about this is *Mistakes Were Made (But not by Me)* by Carol Tavris and Elliot Aronson.[14]

Our deeply held beliefs are created from our experiences, which teach us how to cope with life. Beliefs are thoughts attached to emotions. Emotions are always associated with past experiences. Without the emotions, they would just be thoughts. It is helpful to review my interpretation of the Option Institute's teaching that the formula for everyone's actions is stimulus-belief-response. An event occurs that triggers a belief and then we respond based on the belief. Therefore all events are neutral or just thoughts until we attach an emotion to them, and then the thoughts become beliefs. These beliefs cause us to act in a certain way. We are often called to examine these beliefs when we are struggling, or in pain or depressed.

Our beliefs have developed over the years and we often act without ever recognizing the deeply held beliefs causing our actions. When someone says or does something that we take personally then they have trod upon a deeply held belief and we often react negatively. We can examine the emotions that are attached to a belief, we begin to understand that the belief is just a thought and a thought cannot harm us. We begin to remove the blocks to love's awareness. We can once again access that stately calm within that is with us always but obscured by our beliefs. Now our actions come from this place of peace rather than from unexamined beliefs.

By examining our beliefs we can choose to let go of the emotions that are causing judgment and unhappiness. It is one way to realize that the past no longer has any power to affect us. Through inquiry or questioning our beliefs we can begin the process of understanding how we have used our cherished beliefs to judge ourselves and others who do not share our beliefs. In the larger world we see this happening with science, medicine, religion, and politics. Absolutely everyone uses deeply held beliefs to judge others whether we use traditional or alternative healing methods, or whether we are democrats or republicans, fundamentalist Christians or progressive liberal Christians, or Buddhists or Muslims or any other faith tradition. Realizing this helps in understanding that we are all in this together. Your fears are my fears; your prayer is my prayer.

Gaining an understanding of our deeply held beliefs concerning parenting and our children is critically important or else we may end up trying to control our children or pass on our own insecurities rather than guiding from a place of peace, love, and joy. We teach what we believe. For many parents of children with labels, we think we are unhappy because our child has some type of disorder or disability. In reality our experience always comes from within, from the thoughts and stories we create about our child based on our beliefs. If we are upset and unhappy about the way our children are behaving, it is only because we are seeing our kids and the label they have in ways that are making us upset and unhappy. If we change our thoughts and look at the experience differently, then our actions to our children will change. We can only do this by examining our beliefs. Until we do this, then we act from our insecurities.

When we trust in the internal dialogue or inquiry process then we can begin to truly understand that each one of us, including our children, is always doing the best we can with the awareness we have in any one moment. I used to get hung up on this all the time. I would view my spouse or children as having the information and just refusing to use it. This would trigger my need to control and force them to understand. This is a perfect example of someone who is doing the best they can. I thought I understood this idea, yet, clearly I did not, because I was still using the idea to judge those closest to me.

It took a lot of reading of books, listening to teachers

espousing the same idea but explaining it in different ways, and self examination before I finally had a light bulb go off in my head. Just telling someone something or having them read something does not mean you have caused them to understand it at a deep level. When I added the word *awareness* to the idea, I finally understood. It is immensely freeing to be able to embrace this truth. It allows us to drop assumptions and judgments in order to parent from the heart. It allows us to understand that we can only experience what our thoughts create.

Closely associated with understanding that we are all doing the best we can is the idea that there are no right, wrong, good, or bad thoughts or decisions, just neutral ones. This is a difficult concept to swallow. If thoughts are always associated with concern over past events or worry about the future, then that is true for everyone, even those whose beliefs lead them to cause harm to another. Fear that the results of past events will happen again in the future creates thoughts with emotions that become beliefs that direct behavior. And on the level of form or this physical existence, some behavior is seen as universally more harmful or awful than other behavior. At anybody's level of awareness, we are doing the best we can.

Children, who appear uncontrollable, believe their actions are necessary for their self preservation. Obviously behavior that is harmful to another cannot be allowed and there should be consequences. However the consequences can be administered without succumbing to anger and hate. When we see past the behavior to the light within, then we can begin to understand that the person causing harm was doing the best s/he could with the information and awareness s/he had. Our judgment keeps them in that place of darkness. Seeing with the eyes of God's love illuminates the darkness. People are either expressing love or calling for love, nothing else.[15] When we realize everyone is responding to events based on deeply held beliefs of self preservation, then we can forgive them their actions. In the eyes of

God, we are all innocent.

To Medicate or Not To Medicate

The question of whether or not to medicate your child with a disability or disorder is an excellent example of the concept that there are no right, wrong, good, or bad decisions or events – just thoughts with beliefs attached. Whether to take vitamins, use other alternative healing methods, take prescription medicine and use traditional forms of healing are questions that concern all of us and sometimes cause intense debate among parents of children with labels. It can cause a lot of anguish, particularly among parents with children who have what they call the brain or psychiatric disorders such as: depression, bipolar disorder, schizophrenia, attention deficit disorder, and obsessive compulsive disorder. Whether to medicate or not is also a concern for children within the autism spectrum. The argument is often used that we do not debate whether or not to give insulin to a child with diabetes or antibiotics to a child with pneumonia, why should a child with an emotional disorder be any different? On the level of form, in this physical word, there is a difference between physical illness and what some people call psychiatric or brain disorders. On the level of spirit it is all the same. For a metaphysical discussion about this, please see my chapter on *A Course of Miracles*.

Many adults who have been labeled with autism or ADD do not consider the labels a disorder or disease but a way of being. Many within the psychiatric recovery movement consider bipolar disorder and schizophrenia as psycho-spiritual crises instead of brain disorders and question such a heavy use of medication. The process of inquiry is beneficial for everyone. I return to the idea of seeing past the label to the spirit within. What does it say to your child about being broken when your first and only response is to medicate? The question of medication can derail us from our spiritual journey and fear starts to rule. Some of those long-held beliefs we thought we dropped come back with a vengeance. It is time for self examination.

Like most people, I have spent most of my life believing in the traditional medical models of treatment until I started my spiritual journey with my son. This process led me to totally reject the medical model of treatment. I started by having a lot of angry energy around my new belief that traditional medicine was harmful. I became right and everyone else was wrong. It took a while to release the energy around this belief and accept that it was just a thought with emotions attached. I still believe that we are over medicating our children and that true healing comes through self examination, however, I have dropped the need to be right about this.

The following story illustrates this process.

I have a belief that taking lots of a certain brand of vitamins keeps me healthy. Everyone close to me knows this and periodically tries to change my mind. There has been some recent research supporting the ineffectiveness of vitamins in fighting cancer, which several people close to me were happy to point out and I took it personally. Of course the reason they pointed it out to me was that they have, at times, felt my judgment that they, too, would be healthier taking vitamins.

Taking a certain brand of vitamins is emotional for me because I associate it with healing my debilitating migraines. Therefore, someone challenging my belief that vitamins can heal caused feelings of insecurity. This offered a wonderful opportunity to examine the emotions surrounding the belief, which resulted in finally understanding that "vitamins make you healthy" is just a thought. I created a personal story about taking vitamins and then decided that because it worked for me it must work for everyone. Divest the story of emotions and it becomes just a thought. This does not mean I have to stop taking vitamins and believing they keep me healthy; it means it is no longer personal. I can now release judgments about other people's health beliefs and views and no longer impose my own beliefs. Many of us often decide our life-style choices are the correct way and impose our views on others.

Within my spiritual classroom, alternative approaches to healing my debilitating migraines helped me gain an understanding of being a perfect creation of God. I had my first migraine when I was 10 years old. They continued to escalate in college, graduate school, and beyond. I lost job opportunities because of the migraines. They started with the aura, the blinding zig-zag of light like lightening striking — mostly on one side of my head. I would lose part of my vision, my hands and lips would go numb, and I would get very cold. Then the pain would be so bad, I could not put my head on a pillow. No medication helped, in fact some of it made me more ill. The headache would usually last a day with me lying as quietly as possible and then I would feel wretched the next day. The only thing that helped was drinking massive doses of caffeine. Finally, in my early thirties they discovered that beta blockers worked and my migraines were reduced to one or two a year.

Because of my work with special-needs children, I had become more and more convinced that we are over-medicating our children. This caused me to consider whether I wanted to take beta blockers forever. Eventually I attended a presentation by a nutritionist who talked about diet and vitamin supplements for children with learning differences and attention deficit disorder labels. At the time I found it to be a powerful message that supported the beginning of my belief that our children are not defective, as our labels imply. The program provided a natural alternative, and I was very interested. So I started a supplement program to help with my migraines.

After changing to a more healthy diet and taking supplements for a year, I was eventually able to go off the beta blockers without a massive return of migraines. With this alternative healing regime, I was able to take a good long look at my beliefs concerning health. The thought system behind healthy eating and supplements is based on the concept of wholeness, which provided a new level of awareness that enabled me to start examining the beliefs that were aiding my migraines.

I now realize that I believed I needed the migraines. They were a result of a need to be in control and be perfect at everything I did. They were a release valve for the stress that forced me to quit and rest and everyone in my life was forced to leave me alone. I would get some sympathy and comfort from family and friends. "See how she suffers, isn't she brave..." The lessons I was learning in my spiritual classroom eventually led to a place where, several years ago, when a migraine started, I was able to say to myself, "Sally you do not need this in your life, it is not real, you are whole." And with this thought, the migraine went away and I have not had one since. I do believe that the diseases or physical problems we project into our lives are indicators of what needs to be examined and forgiven.

Part of being in a spiritual classroom is to look at everything in our lives that causes resistance to loving what is, whether it is a person, an event, a sickness, or minor stuff like a stubbed toe. However, we take it too far if we judge ourselves for the sickness or physical problems and then blame ourselves if we cannot heal. It is all part of being in a spiritual classroom and learning to accept whatever happens in our life and be at peace. Accepting what is and listening to the voice of the Unified Spirit instead of the ego will guide us to decisions about whether to medicate or not to medicate. It is all one and the same, a lesson in forgiveness—seeing with the eyes of love and without judgment. So while alternative healing approaches helped me on my journey, they may not be part of your spiritual classroom.

The lesson brings with it an understanding that all of us are doing the best we can with the information and awareness we have at the time. We either choose the ego as our teacher or the Unified Spirit. With the Unified Spirit guiding our inquiry work, we choose, we learn, we gain a new awareness, which brings another choice, which leads to another lesson and awareness and so on and so on until we have removed all the blocks to love's awareness. It is always a spiral upwards. Some people stay stuck for awhile at the bottom of the spiral with the ego as teacher, but eventually everyone will choose the Unified Spirit, God's voice in the world, as their teacher. The Unified Spirit will guide us to symbols or tools that assist with our awareness, just as I was guided to change my diet and use supplements, as I was guided not to use medication for Tyler when he was cutting. You may be guided to using medication for your child or not, it depends on the circumstance.

What is important to remember is that we are whole, spiritual beings having a physical experience. We can recognize this on the level of spirit. On the level of form, we know we are doing the best we can in any given moment. I read a story recently of a father with a child within the autism spectrum who was agonizing over giving medication to his boy. His young child would lash out in rage at various times during the day, hurting anyone near him. Medication helped stop the impulsive rages so that other healing and understanding could occur. Agonizing over giving medication or not giving medication, believing or not believing in the medical model of treatment, is one and the same thing—thoughts with emotions attached. However, it helps to be aware that the medical model repairs the ego.

This does not mean we never take medication or stop our own medication. We observe and are kind to ourselves, and remember we are wholeness of spirit. In some ways it does not matter what form of healing we follow so long as we continue our quest to understand that our bodies are not our reality. So until we remember we are extensions of God's love and thus oneness, we do the best we can in this spiritual classroom, constantly examining our beliefs, trusting and letting go to the Unified Spirit's plan for us.

Awareness is a Process

When we are ready the information becomes awareness. Then with this new level of awareness we will be able to access another level of awareness, but not before we are ready. Therefore we are always doing the best we can with where we are in the moment with whatever level of awareness we are in.

An example of this was my attempts to help Tyler sleep at night. He did not sleep consistently through the night until he was almost eight years old. We tried everything from sympathy, ignoring his crying, no naps during the day, powerful totems, extra lights, soothing bed time stories, and guided meditations. Nothing worked consistently and I was an exhausted parent getting little sleep while trying to be a functioning adult during the day. If I was woken up several times during the night too many nights in a row, I would sometimes yell at him in frustration. A little boy has no need for an angry, yelling mother. Clearly something was going on but I did not know what. It was Tyler who figured it out and if I had been paying attention all the signs were there, I just did not see them because of my own level of understanding.

Sometime during all of this we consulted a psychologist prompted primarily by Tyler's inability to sleep through the night and other concerns. He told us that life for Tyler was like living in grand central station all the time because of sensory integration difficulties. I interpreted this to mean that we should try and eliminate noise in his life so he could concentrate. It feels counter-intuitive to me but Tyler was comfortable with all the noise inside his head. It was silence that scared him. He finally convinced us to let him sleep with music and a fan on. Once we did this he started sleeping through the night.

In retrospect, we would have saved ourselves a lot of sleepless nights and worry, if we had paid attention to what Tyler's actions were telling us. Early on he wanted his door left open so he could hear us talking or the TV going. He often fell asleep immediately and only awakened in terror after we had gone to bed and the house was quiet. Because I cannot sleep unless it is quiet and because of Tyler's sensory integration difficulties, I assumed he needed silence.

To this day, Tyler says he concentrates better with background noise. He deliberately studies and reads in noisy places like Starbucks. He is only now beginning to feel comfortable with silence. When I look back on this period in our lives, I realize we were doing the best we could with the information and awareness we had at the time. Both Tyler and I began to learn to trust his ability to care for himself, rather than the experts and my own assumptions. It does not help to beat myself up for not figuring it out sooner. Instead I realize it was perfect for what we needed to learn in our journey toward understanding.

As parents of children with labels, we often feel as if our lives are made up of constant struggle and problems. However if we choose the Unified Sprit as our teacher instead of the ego then we know that what we are experiencing is perfect for what we need to learn in this spiritual classroom. It always helps to remember that both parent and child are doing the best we can, that the experience is perfect for our spiritual classroom, and that it will lead to a different level of awareness.

I am sure most of us at one time or another has picked up a book to read and it just did not make any sense. Then some time later we feel called to try again and suddenly we understand the book's message. This happened to me with Eckhart Tollé's book, *The Power of Now*. I had the book for several years, periodically looking at it and putting it down unread. Finally one day, I started reading and I understood Tollé's powerful message. Do I judge myself for not having understood earlier? No, I just was not ready. I was doing the best I could at the time with the information I could comprehend. When I was ready, the Unified Spirit guided me to read the book in its entirety. And, when I was ready, the Unified Spirit guided me to read Gary Renard's book, *Disappearance of the Universe*, which taught me about the *Course*. I am still learning about the *Course* teachings. Some ideas I understood immediately, some have come more slowly and clearly. I still have much to understand and forgive in my spiritual classroom.

Sometimes the ego takes over my inquiry work and I blame myself for not feeling more enlightened and being able to see everyone without judgment, with the eyes of God's love. When this happens, it's time to stop, just observe, and be kind to myself, recognizing I am doing the best I can with the awareness I have. Karen Drucker's song, *Gentle with Myself*, has a line I find particularly compelling. "I will only go as fast as the slowest part of me feels safe to go."[16]

This principle works in every aspect of everyone's lives. We are always doing the best we can whether we are open to new possibilities or stuck in our misery, whether we are buried in the ego's thought system or listening to the voice of the Unified Spirit. For people who are committing atrocities and abuse, they are doing the best they can with the awareness they have. This does not mean we excuse or condone their behavior in this physical world. It means we do not judge them. We recognize they have the divine light within as does everyone, but their light is obscured from them and often from us. We recognize they are one with us on the level of spirit, creations of God, and we forgive them for what they cannot see and understand.

This feels really hard. It feels as if we are condoning their destructive behavior. But our judgment only perpetuates their behavior; it is our love for the truth of who they are that will remove the darkness from their eyes so they can see. People are either calling for love or acting from love; people are either living in fear or living in love.[17] The only way to remove the blocks to love's awareness—both for people living in fear and for ourselves—is through non-judgment, recognizing that we are all always doing the best we can with the information and awareness we have in the moment.

Chapter V

The Holy Encounter

When you meet anyone, remember it is a holy encounter.
As you see this person you will see yourself.
As you treat this person you will treat yourself.
As you think of this person you will think of yourself.
Never forget this, for in this person you will find yourself or lose yourself.
Whenever two Offsprings of God meet, they are given another chance at salvation.
Do not leave anyone without giving salvation to them and receiving it yourself.
For I am always there with you, in remembrance of you.

A Course In Miracles, T-142III.4 (Wording changed to be gender neutral)

This physical life is set up so we are constantly bombarded with situations and people who challenge our ability to stay in peace. We often become angry with the people closest to us. It can be someone in the family, our children, our partner, or a friend. In my workshops, I spend a lot of time exploring what to do when children with labels push our buttons. It is time to look within rather than become angry with the child. It is time to go inward and give ourselves the gift of a question.

I say over and over again that it is not about condoning the behavior of the child, it is about embracing the child. People often agree with me or give me puzzled looks. A hard truth to swallow is the idea that we project our own pain and guilt onto other people. It feels as if we are letting the other person off the hook.

70

Again, it is not about condoning behavior but seeing the divine light in every person and embracing his/her divinity. It calls for changing our mind about the person, not fixing the person. After all, can we really ever fix someone? Isn't it their job to understand and heal themselves?

Parents and professionals walk a fine line between supporting and advocating for children and trying to control children's behavior. We justify the control by maintaining they are not old enough to know their own mind. Yet children need adults' belief they are responsible for their own actions and they have the divine wisdom inside—as does everyone—to heal themselves.

If we are all extensions of God's love, then we are part of the one mind. Therefore if we are all one, we meet ourselves over and over again in any encounter with another human being. We meet plenty of people who do not push our buttons and it feels easier seeing them as extensions of God. It is more difficult to see people as extensions of God whose actions are harmful and abusive. We even have difficulty seeing the divine in our family, friends, and everyday acquaintances if we decide that their actions are causing anger or pain.

Actions or words from one person may push my buttons but the same actions and words may not push another person's buttons. Why is this? It is something inside me that needs to be acknowledged and then let go. There is some belief I am holding that results in my anger or upset. It may be a cultural or family belief about how people should act; it may be an old wound from childhood that was never healed. It feels hard to feel a holy encounter with someone whose words or actions are challenging a deeply held belief. Yet how do we feel when we become angry or disgusted with another person's actions or words? We do not feel good, we do not feel peaceful, because when we attack another we attack ourselves.

As I write these words I am mindful of an adult in my life who constantly pushes my buttons as well as everyone else around her. I will call her Jane. She has managed to alienate everyone in the family. The words often used to describe her are all negative: intimidating, controlling, manipulative, prejudiced, does not listen. All of us have challenging people in our lives. I am reminded of a story from L. Tobin from his book, *What Do You Do with a Child Like This?*

Children whom teachers have learned to dislike are the most challenging. Skylar, age six, intimidates adults. See her now with the principal, laughing at him as he scolds her. Or is she?

If the principal looks closely, he will recognize her laughter to be an anxious scream, a mask for the terror she feels. But what strength it takes for him to see through her bizarre laughter to the scared little girl beneath!

Never has a child needed a hug more, and never has an adult been less inclined to offer it.

But he will hug her and the shell will begin to crack.[18]

It does not matter that the difficult person in my life is an adult; I could easily substitute her name for the child in this story. I am sure all of us can substitute names of both adults and children in our lives for the child in this story. We all know adults and children who have become so alienated from their divine, unified self, so dominated by the egoic thought system that it requires infinite patience and a willingness to see their distressing behavior as a call for love rather than taking it personally. Not taking it personally becomes especially difficult when it is our own child. We can easily blame ourselves for our child's struggles or go to the other extreme by dismissing our role in the parent/child relationship.

It feels easier to blame Jane rather than to acknowledge my

thoughts—the thoughts that create the story that she is difficult. After all, it is not just me, everyone else perceives Jane as difficult, so it must be her, not me. The ego is very clever in setting up the situation so that it feels as if it is another person who is the problem, not me. The dynamics of any relationship are really the same; they just feel different because of the physical circumstances. On the level of spirit all relationships are one. Therefore it is through relationship we learn the way back to who we truly are; we are love.

Chickens with Our Heads Cut Off

After a particularly difficult period of time in trying to interact in a peaceful and loving way with Jane, I had a visual epiphany while walking in the woods. I realized that the four members of my family most concerned with Jane were mindlessly running around like chickens with our heads cut off. There she was just being and she would say something or do something and then we would all run around like crazy, not thinking, just reacting. Then there would be a moment of inactivity and we would all calm down and stop running around and then she would say something and we would be mindlessly running around like crazy all over again. We are reacting to her behavior not who she is. She just is, but by reacting like chickens with our heads cut off to her every utterance we are giving her the power to take us out of the truth of who we are. We are giving her the power to take us out of peace.

We do the same with the children we label. We attach labels to children who appear different, thinking that the labels will help us understand how to treat our children so their behavior will be easier to handle. The label gets assigned because of a set of external circumstances and then we imbue the label with the power to upset us. The truth of the child becomes superfluous to the label. We give power to the label and we allow ourselves to mindlessly run around like chickens with our heads cut off every

time the child acts according to the assigned label.

Tobin says, *"The misbehavior of troubled children is seldom what it first appears to be. Understanding this, I believe, is the only place to start. No child has a need to create a life of conflict. Think about it — what need is the child trying to express?"* [19] Can I extend the same belief to someone I perceive as highly difficult? I know Jane is scared, overwhelmed, and very unhappy and I know she has no need for a life of conflict. Out of defense she reacts and attacks because that is how she learned to take care of herself. I can also take all those negative words used about Jane, and come up with more positive words as demonstrated in the reframing exercise in chapter two.

I have also found that the "Loving Kindness" meditation is helpful in releasing judgment of Jane. And so some days, I let it go and compassion comes and then she says and does something that upsets everyone in the family and I get angry, and then I start over again.

Even though I would like to take a giant leap to total forgiveness and love right now, the best I can do is step by step and little by little and then say to myself it is ok, I am doing the best I can and she is doing the best she can and it is as it should be — observing my behavior and hers without judgment. And I am at peace with this. I am reminded of the words from a children's song, "inch by inch, row by row, going to make my garden grow." We do not have to go very far to practice the type of forgiveness described in the holy encounter quote, just our immediate family and friends. And this practice is the same whether it is with an adult or our children.

Suffering and Judgment

I am involved in a letter-writing ministry with a man who is in prison. I will call him Charles. This has been a learning experience for both of us. Charles is evidently a gifted musician who brings joy through sanctioned concerts to the inmates,

prison personnel, and free-world guests. Charles says that he has a diagnosis of bipolar disorder and his letters are filled with thoughts of the abuse he has experienced, particularly from his mother.

This led to an interesting conversation about the purpose of suffering.

This conversation is relevant for this book because a common cultural and religious belief sometimes perpetuated by parents of children with labels is the idea that God blesses us with a child with a disability so we can learn to be better people. This belief is closely associated with the idea that God sent us problems so we can be redeemed through suffering. This is what Charles believes and this is where he stays stuck, reliving the abuse over and over again and using it as a part of a chronicle of abuse, loss, and suffering leading to prison. In this physical world, there is no question that Charles has led a life of tragedy and pain. However, with his thoughts, Charles continues to experience the abuse over and over again in the present. His mother is dead, yet Charles gives her the power, as if she is alive, to abuse him with his continual thoughts of past deeds.

While Charles continues to see suffering as a way to become a better man, he will be unable to rise above it until he understands, "The past is over. It can touch me not."[20] Until Charles can discover the core belief that condemns him to his story of abuse, he will continue to suffer. And of course, being in prison, a soul-deadening place as Charles describes it, provides even more of a challenge to release the suffering. Many parents of children with labels also see themselves as in some type of prison, with no way out. Their child will always have this disability or disorder, it will always be a struggle, and there is no relief. So they stay stuck in pain worrying about what the label implies will be the future for their child.

Some may ask how believing that God sent us problems in order that we may find redemption in suffering, is different from understanding that we are in a spiritual classroom in which every event is an opportunity to learn forgiveness? However, there is a profound distinction between believing God sent us problems so we can learn through suffering and recognizing that our belief in separateness from God creates our problems, and then finding grace in the midst of suffering. WM. Paul Young writes in his novel, *The Shack*, "Grace doesn't depend on suffering to exist, but where there is suffering you will find grace in many facets and colors."[21] This is what it means to be in a spiritual classroom, finding grace to transcend the suffering caused by our belief in separation from God's eternal love.

I have had conversations with thoughtful, spiritually minded friends about whether they feel separated from God or not. Most say they do not. We think we have a relationship with God, one based on trust and love, but do we? If we did not believe in separation, we would embody God's unconditional love on earth. Most of us are not there yet. We have a troubling relationship with God: we judge or reject God or we ask God to be judge and play favorites.

The evidence that we believe in separation confronts us over and over again whenever we judge ourselves or another person. When we judge others, we are actually judging ourselves because we are one with God. This judgment perpetuates the belief in separation; believing God judges us we fear God's judgment. So we project our judgments onto others to show God we are innocent and that it is someone else's fault. This becomes a never-ending cycle of judgment and suffering. All of us have suffered; it is the way the ego works. God's unconditional love working through us as the voice of the Unified Spirit breaks this cycle of judgment and suffering. It allows us to create a circle of love instead, to remove the blocks to love's awareness and embody God's unconditional love on earth.

We try to make God into our image of a judging person. We say: stop this, do this, love this person, punish that person, stop my child's suffering, stop my suffering. We judge God for allowing all the wrongs in the world and then when stuff goes wrong as it always does, we think God cannot be trusted. The only judgment God makes is everyone, absolutely everyone, is worthy of love.

Another way to look at this is through our love for our children. I would guess most parents reading this book feel they love their children unconditionally at least most of the time. And because many of us have a child with a label, we have learned to treat each of our children differently based on their unique strengths and needs.

What would we do if we were asked to treat one of our children harshly or to sacrifice one to someone else's abuse? We would not do it. Why then would we expect God, who loves us unconditionally, to make such a choice to give a child a disability or to sacrifice one to abuse? This not the truth because God is not of this world. God is in this world only in our remembrance of being one with God, our higher unified self, the voice of the Unified Spirit.

Your Light Is All I See

I love the words from the African Amercan spiritual, "This little light of mine, I'm gonna let it shine." It conveys so much of what I wish for all our children. We use many symbolic words of light as a way to describe the mystery of the divine. Phrases about light and images of light are constantly tumbling around in my mind and pop into my brain at odd moments, especially when I need encouragement. They are: "go forth and be a light unto the world", "do not hide your light under a bushel", "the light has come", "I'd rather light a candle than curse the darkness", and "the unbearable lightness of being".

We often use the image of light burning away the darkness of the soul, or lighting one's way out of the darkness of confusion. Just one glimpse of the sun on a cloudy, rainy day can lighten my mood. When we are confused we often use the phrase, "I now see the light" to express an end to confusion or a dawning realization.

In my presentations, I talk about seeing the inner divine light in every child no matter the behavior or disabling condition. I want to be able to see that inner light in every person I meet, no matter how buried or faint it appears to be. In Karen White's novel, *Pieces of the Heart*, a friend says to another friend, "I wish I could show you, when you are lonely or in darkness, the astonishing light of your own being."[22] The essence of the holy encounter is holding the divine light or the love of God in every person we meet and in ourselves.

What is this light? It is our remembrance of being one with God that is the inner light that shines in every person, absolutely every person. God is light; God is love. Our inner light is an internal reminder of God's presence and God's love in us, working through us always.

What does it mean to see the light in our children, our partner, our family, and friends? What does it mean to see the light even in people who are doing great wrong and committing violent acts out of fear, anger, or revenge? Is it possible to still see God's light in them, to embrace this light? Embracing does not mean condoning terrible acts or even minor irritations or judgments; it means trusting that God's love is in every person and this is all that matters. Their light may be dim and flicker but it will never go out. God's love cannot be quenched. God only sees wholeness of spirit because we are one with Him/Her. We move away from our remembrance that we are one with God, when we fail to see the light in every living being. We let the darkness in when we judge or attack another. *A Course In Miracles* asks that we practice this thought, "The light has come. I have forgiven the world."[23] Can we do no less than forgive our belief in separation when God forgives us?

Jerald Jampolsky's words about light become my prayer to

remember to say to every person I meet, to every politician who upsets me, to every person consumed by hatred, to my children and spouse, "Your light is all that I see and is but a reflection of the light in me."[24] And when our children are struggling to be seen as whole instead of broken, to say, "I wish I could show you, when you are lonely or in darkness, the astonishing light of your own being."[25]

This little light of mine,
I'm gonna let it shine.

Chapter VI

Trust, Let Go and Surrender

Do you have the patience to wait
Till your mud settles and the water is clear?
Can you remain unmoving
Till the right action arises by itself?
–Lao-tzu, *Tao Te Ching*

Closely associated with the idea that every person we meet or have a relationship with is a holy encounter, is the ability to trust. Trust that the Unified Spirit is working through you, your child, through every single person, no matter how deep he or she seems to be in the ego's darkness. Trust that grace can be found in suffering, "till your mud settles and the water is clear," in other words, till your dark thoughts are released and your mind is still. Trust requires patience to wait, to accept what happens as meant to happen.

Letting go of the thoughts that create a story of suffering means accepting what is, trusting that whatever arises is as it is supposed to be. Trusting in the Unified Spirit's plan, letting go of thoughts that create suffering, surrendering to the moment — these do not necessarily happen in order. They are not linear concepts. Sometimes we have to let go before we can trust, sometimes we have to take a leap and trust in order to let go, sometimes we have to surrender to "the dark night of the soul" before we can let go and then trust.

Essential to trusting, letting go and surrendering is patience, the patience to wait, to just be, holding constantly the thought that what is happening is supposed to happen and there is always a light in the darkness of your suffering. When we are in the midst of difficult times with our child, patience can feel in short supply. We can consider being patient with the everyday irritations, but how can we possibly have patience when our child needs an immediate life-saving operation, or our child's constant raging leaves us too exhausted, or our child is contemplating suicide?

Time is the ego's invention to keep us obsessing about the past and worrying about the future. All that exists is the present moment. We cannot stop the thoughts from intruding in the present moment; however, we can meet them with understanding through our inquiry work and realize they cannot affect us. So if a situation seems immediate, take a look at your thoughts. Our response to a crisis can be met with calmness when we realize it is our thoughts about what has happened in the past that are creating a worry about the future. The perfect answer just appears when we stay present.

When Tyler was depressed and cutting, and Rick and I were struggling with our marriage, and my father died, I was so overwhelmed I just gave up trying to control what was happening. It was so much easier to surrender to the moment and trust that all was happening as it should. And when I surrendered to what was, I felt immense grace, which manifested as detachment to what was happening, even while I was in the midst of struggling with the pain and anger.

It is difficult to explain how calm I felt amidst all the suffering I was experiencing. I just trusted that the Unified Spirit was in charge, not me, and that my family and I would emerge in a better place, no matter the outcome. There was nothing I could do but live moment to moment. And I observed that I suffered whenever I allowed myself to worry about Tyler's or my future and when I judged my husband. When I stayed present, not judging, just accepting what was happening, I stayed calm and I felt grateful for events as they unfolded.

While I learned a lot about how our thoughts cause our

suffering, after the crisis passed, I found myself slipping back into the old routine of thinking I can control what happens in my life, occasionally worrying about what if, and trying to stop what if, before it happened. It is often a crisis that forces us to trust, let go, and surrender. And because our labeled children are often the catalyst for crises, we get thrown into situations over and over again that bless us with the opportunity to accept whatever happens, stay present, trust and let go. Releasing judgment automatically keeps us in the present and we realize that suffering is only in our mind. A *Course in Miracles* says that we are not victims of the world we see.[26]

Another time I became so overwhelmed I just let go and stayed in the moment was when my mother died. There was so much to do with my work, closing my mother's house, my daughter's graduation from college, upcoming holidays, that I let go trying to control and anticipate. And it all got done without any worry. Emails or people appeared, reminding me to take care of tasks without any planning or scheduling. It was immensely freeing to just let go and trust.

So, given these two times of living in the moment, why would I want to go back to the old way of anticipating problems or trying to create opportunities and then planning and scheduling so they do or do not happen? Why does it take a crisis to catapult me into accepting what is? It's the everyday stuff that can take us quickly out of peace because it becomes a routine and it feels easy to fall back into old habits. When this happens, I remind myself to let go, and I will stop and think of one moment of joy in my day to take me back to peace.

Recently a large fundraising event someone else was organizing was cancelled. I thought this fundraiser was critical for raising the money necessary for a conference I was planning. Because my nonprofit organization was on the hook to the hotel for some money if the conference did not take place, I panicked. I did not meet with any understanding all the thoughts that crowded into my head about financial disaster and all those people who depended on me not to fail. I was also battling feelings of being a failure. Slowly I remembered to do my inquiry work and to realize I had no idea what was supposed to happen, they were just thoughts. When we get pulled out of the present, believing the disaster or failure story our thoughts are creating, we let in fear, which chokes out any possibility of allowing the answer to arise.

The ego is really clever about trapping us with our own misunderstanding of forgiveness lessons. I thought that if financial disaster was a forgiveness lesson, I had no desire to experience it. However, gradually I regained my sanity, talked to various people, and refocused on enjoying each day, trusting it would work out the way it was supposed to, no matter the outcome. I even feel peaceful with the final decision to cancel the conference, an event I invested a lot of time and energy planning over several years. And it all worked out with the hotel releasing us from the financial contract.

If I am going to get really stuck and then panic, it is around money. I think this is probably true for a lot of us. One issue that comes up over and over again with parents is how expensive it is to have a child with a label. Doctors, therapists, specialists, special programs, day-care attendants, and special schools are all so expensive. I know parents who have become almost bankrupt with paying for all the services their child needs. Often we can trust the process until it comes to money, then we get derailed. There is a lot more fear associated with lack of money than with a failed relationship. Lack of money conjures up thoughts of being unable to pay bills, going into debt, losing all we own, not having the life we want, and maybe living on the street. Once again they are thoughts of the future, which take us out of peace.

The process is the same for every distressing event, trust in the Unified Spirit's voice in the moment, let go of judgments, meet our thoughts of disaster with understanding, and surrender to God's plan for us. In the stillness of the moment we know we are safe and loved. It takes lots of inquiry work when we are worried about money. It is a great invention of the ego to keep us in fear. And once in fear all the creative solutions dry up. It takes one tiny step at a time, breathe, meditate, and just observe the thoughts that come through that keep you in fear. Eventually, by just observing, there will be shifts in awareness, and creative solutions will appear.

Who Would You Be without Your Story

Think about it, who would we be without our story of being a parent, a parent of a child with a label, a spouse or partner, a friend, a woman, a man? When we think about a person, an object, or ourselves, we are thinking about the past. It is the only way we know to identify the object or the person. Our thoughts then re-tell and re-create the story of the person or object always in the present. Therefore in the present we have the infinite opportunity to meet a person as if *for the first time* without their story.[27] This is the heart of accepting what is: recognizing that the past is over and has no power to affect us in the present unless we choose the ego as our teacher. Without our story of the past, would we be able to see each person as if *for the first time*; would we be the unconditional love of God?[28]

We are attached to our story of individuality. We think it defines who we are, a special person with our gifts and weaknesses. We use our story as a defense against the truth. We use our story to stop looking at what it really means to end our judgment of others. If we saw them as if *for the first time* without their stories (our thoughts of the past) then we would see ourselves *for the first time* without our story. How scary is that? Who would I be without my story? Would I be left with just the eternal light of God? How scary becomes miraculous.

An example of what it feels like to be without our story of being a parent confronts us when our children leave home for the first time to be on their own either at college or the military or a self-sustaining job. Every year in August, the internet, the newspapers, and magazines are filled with advice on how to survive when your child goes to college. Clearly this is a universal lesson to accepting what is for many of us in our spiritual classroom called parenting.

When my daughter Sarah went to college for the first time, I literally felt as if I had been punched in the stomach. And I have to laugh because I thought I was so well prepared, after all, I was on a spiritual parenting journey, I taught this stuff. I thought I knew what to do to avoid the empty-nest feeling. It felt even worse because my highly independent daughter, who had spent every summer since age ten away from home, was terribly homesick for the first time. I knew that the best way to help Sarah was to heal my own pain. I realized I had become attached to the daily activity of parenting, the role of being Sarah's mother. The panic came from not knowing who I would be without this story.

I realized I was in a major transition period in my life and transitions are often the most painful because we have no idea where we are going. Transition periods are unsettling because a story has ended and we allow ourselves to get pulled out of the present by our worry of who we will be in the future. Sometimes the best I could do was escape the feeling entirely by reading a murder mystery or watching a movie. Six hours of the TV production of *Pride and Prejudice* worked nicely.

It took several weeks of inquiry work before the endless panic I was feeling disappeared. I experienced this again although to a lesser degree when Tyler left for college. So it is a process. It is a lesson most parents experience. And it is an excellent opportunity to examine our beliefs to learn to accept what is. We gradually learn that when we become so attached to one role, accepting whatever happens becomes difficult and we are taken out of peace.

Who would you be without your story of parenting a child

with a label? Who would you be without the story of: my child has autism, bipolar disorder, attention deficit disorder, cerebral palsy—any of the disability labels? We often believe that the more positive labels will allow us to parent from a place of peace. However, who would you be without your story of my child is intellectually gifted, or creative, or adventurous, or any culturally positive labels? What would happen if we met our children each day as if *for the first time*?

Perhaps we would see with the eyes of love in one holy instant.

Given that most of us are not yet able to totally comprehend our projection of fears and judgments onto others, being able to see our children with fresh eyes as if *for the first time* may be all we can accomplish in any given moment. But it is a positive step. If we could see our child with fresh eyes, then we might be able to see how the story of autism, or dyslexia, or any label including the positive ones, is limiting our children to our perceptions. Our thoughts about a label, thoughts that are based on the past that does not exist anymore, automatically pre-determine our response to our child. The disability labels conjure up struggle, differences, fear of the future — all of which get assigned to our child and then it becomes a self-fulfilling prophecy. Would you parent your child differently if he or she did not have this label attached? Would you parent your child differently if each moment you looked at him or her with fresh eyes, as if *for the first time*?

I can feel the ego in me saying, "Get real, you, your family, your friends, everyone is attached to the stories they create. So even if you can see your child each day with fresh eyes, the rest of the world does not and your child has to survive, so you have to play the game." It really does not matter what everyone else is thinking or doing, all that matters is your decision to choose the Unified Spirit as your teacher; your decision to look at your child with fresh eyes.

I cannot emphasize too much what a shift in parenting will

occur when you move from worry, to accepting what is, to unconditional love. It brings us back to trusting the process, letting go to the voice of the Unified Spirit, and surrendering to whatever happens. When we surrender and give up trying to control, we know what to do. It is a shift in attitude, a shift in understanding, a few more obstacles removed in our awareness of love. It cannot be explained; words are just symbols. It is intuitive. You understand when it happens. So until it does, we choose over and over again the Unified Spirit as our teacher instead of the ego's thought system of projection, guilt, and suffering.

Every painful and stressful event in my life has led to greater understanding, one step closer to full forgiveness, and more peace in my heart. Why would any painful or stressful event I may still encounter be any different? Why would I be afraid? Instead I can say to myself, "I am safe, I am learning what I am supposed to learn—it is perfect for what I need right now and it leads to a more peaceful and loving way of being. Each step leads me closer to being one with God and I am joyful that I am going home. I embrace each stressful or resistant thought as it is a means for my release and return to God. I cannot know the outcome. I can only trust it will be perfect for understanding the Unified Spirit's lessons in forgiveness. This is the ultimate trust that no matter the outcome, it is perfect for my lesson in forgiveness."

If you are stuck in your children's story, banging your head against the wall of judgments, pain, and struggle, ask yourself what would happen if you saw your child as if *for the first time*, with fresh eyes, without all the garbage that comes with the label. Then you need infinite patience and trust that this new seeing will gradually change you and your child to act from a place of love. You will need to be constantly vigilant not to get pulled back into the label's story because the ego, in the guise of everyone else, will constantly try to drag you down.

Courage does not come from fighting the system, trying to fix your child, and control the outcome; courage is surrendering to the moment, seeing your child as if *for the first time*. Courage is having the patience to wait "…till the mud settles and the water is clear," remaining calm with no need to control the current, surrendering to the flow, "till the right action arises by itself."

Chapter VII

I Can Have Peace Instead of This;
Parents' Stories

*I used to know an old man who could walk by any cornfield and hear
the corn singing.*
*"Teach me," I'd say when we'd passed on by. (I never said a word
while he was listening.)*
"Just tell me how you learned to hear that corn."
And he'd say, "It takes a lot of practice. You can't be in a hurry."
And I'd say, "I have the time."
–Byrd Baylor, *The Other Way to Listen*

Parenting is really about an opportunity to look at yourself. I
cannot begin to count the numerous times my relationship with
my children has led to self examination and an important
spiritual learning. If we are willing to listen and if we have
infinite patience, our children will teach us to hear the singing of
our inner voice — the voice of the Unified Spirit, our higher
unified self. Most parents realize they have signed on for life to
be a parent. Therefore, we do not have to hurry; we have plenty
of time to learn to listen.

Both my children are now in their twenties, and they still
continually teach me how to listen and learn. Sarah is struggling
to find her place in the world physically, emotionally, and spiritually. I want to give her all the wisdom I've learned. I want her to
follow my spiritual path. But that is arrogant and unproductive. I
cannot short circuit her spiritual journey. I cannot presume to
know her path. So I am learning to listen more and instruct less,
just asking questions in order to guide her self-examination. I need
to remember that the best gift I can give to my daughter is to

refrain from telling her what to do because I trust that she will find her own way to the peace that lies within her.

Recently there was a cartoon in the Boston Globe's *Parade* magazine that captures this idea perfectly. It shows a mother and father sitting on a couch looking at what I presume is their college-age child. The father says, "What's the point of taking time off to find out who you are when your mother and I can just tell you?"[29]

Two of the ways Tyler worked through his depression and cutting was through writing poems and creating his art. He wrote and expressed a lot of anger and despair, which eventually led to more positive messages and to him becoming spiritually grounded. Now Tyler is secure in his spiritual path, open and questioning. He says that he is not religious but he is faith-driven. However, Tyler still often expresses the darkness in his poems and art. I allowed myself to worry that by expressing the darkness and pain over and over again, he would be drawn back into it. He assured me this was not the case, that his dark poems helped him work through his feelings. This is a good example of how I let thoughts of past events create worry. Tyler always teaches when I am willing to listen. The following email from Tyler and my response is an example of this.

Hey Mom:

You know how I've been trying to explain to you for the longest time why some of the things I write come across dark or negative? I don't know how you described it, but yeah, sometimes I do write some of my stuff with a positive message but last night I came up with something with the exact words that I've been trying to tell you on why I sometimes express those dark emotions in writing. And I'm really proud of it, so I wanted to show you so then maybe you'd understand why I express all those darker emotions in my writing. It's not because I am negative or that my life is dark, which I know you know, but it's because it helps me get to hope in a different and more satisfying way, sometimes rather than just going ahead and expressing the positive when I do not feel it yet. Here it is:

It's good to be bitter and broken sometimes because that's when the most powerful emotions are expressed. And those lead you to hope when all light is dim. There is power in expressing and getting out deep emotions of bitterness, especially in a healthy manner because that is how we heal ourselves.

Love, Ty

Dearest Tyler:

Thank you for sharing your thoughts and what you wrote about darker emotions. I totally agree with what you are saying. When I would talk to you about not dwelling on the negative, it came out of fear that you would get stuck in the negative. I saw my bright boy over many years gradually slide into depression. It was a long slide and at times I did not realize it was happening. It was when you started cutting that both of us realized how bad it had become. Out of that darkness and struggle you emerged once again as your bright radiant self only now with a deeper understanding of the human condition and with a capacity to love the divine in every person.

So I also believe what you wrote so beautifully, "It's good to be bitter and broken sometimes because that's when the most powerful emotions are expressed. And those lead you to hope, when all light is dim."

There is a book by Miriam Greenspan I recommend to people who are going through difficult times called *Healing Through the Dark Emotions*. Sadness, pain, and despair turn into joy when we are willing to work through these dark emotions. If we trust in the process and believe that there is always a light at the end of the dark, lonely tunnel, then we will always come through whatever struggles we face. What happens is people get stuck in the darkness and fall in love with it and sometimes never emerge.

So when I would suggest you write about the positive in your poems, I was acting from a place which was afraid you would get stuck again in the darkness. I know I need to trust and let go and know every person is on their own spiritual journey and have their own lessons to learn. I do not have the larger picture, only God has that. Usually I can do this, however it is sometimes more difficult for a mother to let go and trust the process when it is her child who is struggling.

Life will never be perfect. The ego-self will always make sure that something goes wrong. However according to *A Course in Miracles* we can either choose to see the world as a prison and stay stuck or see the world as a classroom with each difficult life event as an opportunity to learn to forgive our thoughts of separation and return home to our true selves as extensions of God's love. We do not search for God's love; our life's lessons are to remove the obstacles which keep us from realizing that we are already love. I have had my own struggles this summer. So thank you for your words of wisdom to help bring me back to knowing I will emerge from this with another large obstacle removed to love's awareness. You are the face of God; we are all the face of God.

Love and blessings, Mom

Parents' Stories

The role of parent changes over time as our children grow. However, sometimes with our labeled children, it feels as if the struggles are never ending, one struggle is resolved only to be replaced by another. On the level of form, it can feel like a roller coaster ride of problems, pain, grief, sadness, and normalcy over and over again.

One of my clients, Katie, whose story is included here, expressed it this way. "The most useful image of grief for me is of a spiral. The person moves up and down the spiral in intensity and suffering. Fear, anger, frustration, hopelessness, helplessness, and loneliness recur on the curves. Parents do not go through stages of grief because stages suggest a fixed sequence and an ending. This is not useful because parents of kids with labels do not complete stages to move on. They are always just an incident away from renewed, intense grief. The unproductive situation like mine was 'frozen grief' because I was stuck in it." Once we accept that this is what happens to many parents of children with labels, then the only thing we can do is figure out how to be at peace, no matter what is happening around us, so that we do not engage in the roller coaster ride or stay stuck in "frozen grief".

The following are stories of parents who are in different stages in the process of being able to do this. You may see yourself in some of these stories. These parents show immense courage to look within, listen to their children, and only then find a way to parent from the heart and from peace.

The first story is about Katie. I met Katie at one of my workshops. She joined my email list and when I announced I was offering personal phone consultations, she called and we started talking. At the time I started working with Katie, she was in the stage of what she termed "frozen grief". When I asked her to write her story for this book, she had finally found some peace and did not want to go back and re-view old emotions. So instead, she sent some basic notes and based on what I already knew about Katie, I wrote her story.

The next two stories are from sisters, Deirdre and Mary Pat, who participated in my spiritual parenting workshops. In these workshops they learned about the Option Institute and the Son Rise Program primarily for children within the autism spectrum, which I mention in chapter three. Both have experienced the benefits of internal dialogue in accepting their labeled children with joy. Both have used the parenting experience to deepen their love and understanding of their relationship with God.

Katie

When Katie and her husband adopted siblings, a boy and a girl, Katie expected life would evolve in a normal way. Her children would have the usual problems growing up but nothing dramatic. Katie and her husband would both have careers and also take time to raise their children. But that is not what happened.

Starting when he was a toddler, Spencer had problems with self-control, social relationships, attention, and energy. Consistently over several years, Katie was asked to remove him from schools, activities, and sports teams. Katie felt their home life was a nightmare where the family was sad, angry, overwhelmed, and discouraged.

From the time Spencer was five years old, they sought professional help, to no avail. No one seemed to understand Spencer's problems or how to fix them. Depending on the professional, different labels were assigned, including: Asperger's syndrome, attention deficit hyperactive disorder, attachment disorder, bipolar disorder, emotionally disturbed, and gifted. Spencer participated in counseling and took medications. But Spencer would curl up in his room and talk about wanting to die, which just made it feel worse to his parents.

Katie and her husband attended training for special-needs

children. Spencer's younger sister was in psychotherapy to cope with a brother who alternately withdrew and frightened her. Katie attended a grief counseling workshop to deal with the loss of her dream family. She was also in psychotherapy to address her anger and helplessness. Nothing worked to fix their beloved son and to lessen Katie's suffering.

Feeling they had no choice, Katie and her husband placed Spencer for 18 months in a residential treatment center for emotionally disturbed boys in a state far from their home. Katie mourned that Spencer turned 12 years old away from his family. Katie was unhappy with Spencer's progress and once again needed to move him to another school in a part of the country even farther away from their home. Once again she felt betrayed by the professionals who said they could help her son. It was after this move to a new therapeutic boarding school that I started talking with Katie and helping her engage in self examination. During this time, Spencer began making progress in self control, making and keeping friends, accepting adult guidance, and being a productive student. Katie reports that he has found his passion in cross-country running and earned a school trip to Africa.

Katie plans to keep Spencer in this school for two years but has no idea what to expect beyond that. They travel long distance to the school several times a year to take him away for weekends. Spencer comes home for school holidays. They are long-distance parents and Katie says that the financial and emotional resources and time required to live this way are tremendous. Even though she loves her son, Katie was frustrated and at times resentful that she had to put her life and career on hold to care for Spencer. This is not how she saw her life unfolding. This was not what she signed up for.

When I started talking with Katie, she expressed intense grief and loss about what her life with "normal" children could have been. The words Katie used to describe how she felt were despair, sadness, loneliness, hopelessness, worried about the future, and she was obsessed about Spencer's past. With her thoughts, Katie relived the past trauma over and over again in the present and expected the future to continue the same painful way. This was keeping her "frozen in grief".

One of the areas I worked with Katie was discovering the beliefs that were keeping her suffering and unhappy. She worked hard at uncovering the following self-limiting or unproductive beliefs. I am sure many of us at some time or another have held similar self-limiting beliefs.

- ✓ Experts know what they are doing and they can fix my son.
- ✓ Our nurturing environment will overcome his wiring defects.
- ✓ Big effort produces good outcomes or results.
- ✓ Understanding of problems leads to effective intervention/action.
- ✓ If I don't suffer with my child or worry about him, then I don't care about him.
- ✓ I must arrange my life to minimize stress, anxiety, and loss.
- ✓ This will never end.
- ✓ I am a sad, negative, worrier who has finally found a problem worthy of me.
- ✓ I should get what I planned and worked for. Life should be fair.
- ✓ I must look at the past and fear the future to be sure I'm doing the right thing in the present.
- ✓ What others think of my children matters to me. Kids are a reflection of their parents.
- ✓ I must feel good emotionally and physically to do something challenging.
- ✓ I am a professional failure.
- ✓ I am the wrong mother. He is the wrong child and he has ruined my life.

✓ We are idiots for adopting, for failing to heed warnings about the higher incidence of problems of adopted children.

✓ We were naïve to think our resources and love could conquer all.

In summary, Katie felt all her expectations about the world, life, mental health and child rearing were violated. We can read her beliefs and understand why they kept Katie in a cycle of grief and suffering. We can also understand how each one of those beliefs can keep one in their grip. The problem in holding so strongly to long-held cherished beliefs is that life (or the ego) will always find a way to challenge your belief. We often hold even more tightly to cherished beliefs when we feel threatened because at some point in the past we thought they served us. Our cherished beliefs gave us the illusion that we were in control of our life. When we realize they are not working, we can become, as Katie put it, "frozen in grief," unable to let go of the unproductive beliefs and afraid to move on for terror of the unknown.

The process of finding a way to be at peace no matter what is happening to your child or to you, usually begins when you say to yourself, "This is intolerable, there has to be another way." This lets in the voice of the Unified Spirit to be your teacher, to guide you toward approaches and symbols you can understand. Going inward is a huge and courageous step for any of us to uncover those beliefs that keep us suffering. Sometimes just uncovering a belief allows us to see the insanity, and the belief just disappears. Sometimes it takes much more self inquiry to drop a self-limiting belief.

The belief Katie has had the most difficulty dropping, and that drives all her beliefs is, "This is not the life I was supposed to have." By constantly holding tight to the belief that the life she has is not the one she signed up for, this has kept her imprisoned in unhappiness, with the inability to appreciate what was good in her life. When we see that the life we have is perfect for what we need to learn, then we start to see the blessings, we start being able to listen to the voice of the Unified Spirit, we start being grateful for being in a spiritual classroom.

Through much self-examination, Katie began to realize she was angry and grieving over past events that she could not change and worrying about Spencer's and her future, which she could not control. The process of inquiry allows us to uncover the beliefs that are causing us to suffer and then just let them be. As we observe and do nothing but acknowledge our self-limiting beliefs, they are eventually released as having no power to affect us.

Katie still believes that watching her child suffer for years is a unique hell and she has lost a lot along the way. With continued self examination Katie will be begin to realize that her life has unfolded perfectly for what she needs to learn in this spiritual classroom. She has begun the process of using the experience to grow spiritually, learn lessons and acquire tools for living. She says that now she is living more in the present, searching for calm no matter what happens around her.

Katie is happy to be Spencer's mother because she and her husband can help him become his best self and in the process, become their best selves — patient, compassionate, and hopeful. She also believes her marriage has become stronger from parenting Spencer. These are more useful beliefs than believing that parenting Spencer was a mistake. She is learning to be grateful for the life she has and to create a more positive parenting story. Through self-examination, and by cultivating spiritual practices such as prayer and meditation, and getting support from other mothers of children with labels, Katie has freed herself to find a passion in horses, and appreciate a daughter who has typical adolescent struggles.

Katie is beginning to realize that peace lies within as she accepts the flow of spirit in her life. She is beginning to realize she is always doing the best she can with the awareness she has in each moment. She cannot control or fix Spencer, she can only change how she feels; she can only change her mind about the situation. Katie continues to guide and advocate for Spencer, only now, more and more, she does it from a place of calm rather than anger and grief. It frees Spencer to be who he is without feeling the burden of his mother's despair. As Katie and Spencer create a more positive, loving story they will more often choose the Unified Spirit as their teacher. Accepting what is, is now a journey both can experience.

Deirdre

It's a boy!!!! My husband and I, along with our four daughters, welcomed another new baby into our lives. The excitement sent vibrations through the room as each one of us cuddled and held him. His impact on our family was immediate. Our happiness was tested instantly when Kevin was suspected of having a possible chromosome disorder. However, it was not until December of 2009, some 11 years later, that Kevin was diagnosed at Boston Children's Hospital as having chromosome 16q deletion, together with a dual diagnosis of autism. The experience of being Kevin's mother has been my greatest source of spiritual growth.

What if you thought you were happy and found out you really weren't; what if you thought you were spiritual and then discovered it was all just perception? I told everyone I met that Kevin was a gift... but when I told my story, the sadness and emotion would sometimes make it difficult to speak.

My perception began to change while attending a program at the Option Institute called "Happiness is a Choice." I was attending with my daughter who was feeling very unhappy. As I explained the weekend's upcoming events to some friends, someone commented, "Well, you have always had a great attitude, your glass is always half full." Ah yes, glass half full was a positive thing because after all, I was facing a lot of adversity. I proudly accepted the compliment.

At the Option Institute I began to re-think my life and re-evaluate what happiness is. Don't forget, I thought I already was happy. I soon realized my happiness was just a perspective. If I was happy and I felt that Kevin was a gift, then why would I be brought to tears with just the mere mention of his struggles? When was the last time you cried with sadness upon receiving your best gift? Awakening to this idea was definitely the turning point in my life. I realized that my beliefs formed my perspective.

Later in the year I returned to the Option Institute for training in the Son Rise Program®. This program is designed to help children with disabilities become their best selves in the most loving of atmospheres. I learned many techniques and ways to engage Kevin on his terms, trusting he knows best for himself.

While I was there I remembered the words, "Your glass is always half full." Who in their right mind would ever settle on having their glass half full when it is possible to have your glass full? If your glass is half full, it is based on your belief that you lack something others have. I had been unaware, but I now realized that I had this belief. I believed deep down that I had been given less and that there had been a big mistake. I did not believe that Kevin was a mistake, but rather that the whole situation had gone wrong.

It was a workshop with Sally that helped me see my life as present perfection. I see each day as an opportunity to look at my beliefs and to this day they are unfolding. Each day brings new perspectives and opportunities to see the world as coming *from* me, not *at* me. I am my world and it is my choice to see each life event as a spiritual lesson. Perfection is flawless, as is God's love... constant and unconditional.

If I had advice for a parent it would be this...You need only to let go of one belief to begin this journey... Let go of the idea that the events in front of you are your reality. They are not your reality. Your beliefs create your reality. As you unravel your beliefs, your perception of reality changes and you begin to see life as it should be, one of infinite possibilities.

This journey continues, but I am so glad to be living in a state of grace. A friend once asked me, "What exactly is GRACE?" After thinking for a while, I came up with this: GRACE; the "GR" represents gratitude and the "ACE" represents peace. Living in gratitude for all that comes your way and then through forgiveness, and the unraveling of your beliefs, you have peace which brings to light GRACE.

Mary Pat

The spiritual lessons I have learned while raising my children have been many. These are some of my thoughts. What if, in this benevolent universe, earth is the ultimate playroom? What if, just as our children in the Son-Rise playroom have this most accepting therapy program, which allows for choices, we also have the option to choose how engaged we want to be in our world? We have the most effective therapy available for ourselves, one based on being accepting, loving, and nonjudgmental of OURSELVES, especially if we choose to see the universe as benevolent, loving, accepting, and nonjudgmental. WOW, life is a boundless, enormous Son-Rise program! I can laugh joyfully in my mind at this analogy. I do bring a lot of joy to myself when I understand my life this way.

My journey began with the birth of my twin son and daughter, who were each born with Down syndrome and recently also diagnosed with autism. What if I choose to become "awake" to this whole idea of being the creator of my life experiences by deciding I will create a huge, undeniable, rare event for myself by giving birth to twins with Down syndrome? They are unique as fraternal twins with Down syndrome, as verified by the leading expert at Boston's Children's Hospital. Of course, with a blessing like this occurring in my life, I have created a most wonderful opportunity to choose how to experience my children with special needs and how to experience myself as a mother and wife. Do I choose to see how terribly disappointing or how wonderfully exciting this is?

I wanted to be happy and at peace with my life, happy in my marriage, and as a mom. Once my twins arrived, for the very first time I felt my dream was gone. Life became a burden and difficult and the worry was unbearable. Would the three holes in my daughter Marion's heart require surgery? Would her inflamed kidney correct itself or lead to bladder infections and eventually, surgery? Was it possible she was blind, since her eyes never focused on a fixed item? Would my son Sean's laser surgery for severe laryangomalcia be successful? Will I ever have time for my older son Nuccio? Will I ever get a full night's rest? Will I ever have time or the desire to be with my husband in a romantic way again? Can I handle the tremendous work involved in caring for my children, such as the countless diaper changes, the endless meal preparations, and the unbelievable amount of clean-up after meal time spills? After four years of living like this, I reached an all-time low. Do I leave my husband? He was so unhappy with me, and with life. I definitely saw a change in his outlook on life after the twins were born, but I did not see that the same change was in me. I was unhappy, depressed, and exhausted.

At Sally's workshop, "Parenting as a Spiritual Journey," I considered more deeply why my children were in my life. I knew my kids were gifts and that God does not make mistakes, but what did all this mean? Did Sean, Marion, and Nuccio choose me to be their mom? Did I choose them to be my children? Then I heard about the *Son Rise* story, *the Miracle Continues* about Raun Kaufman from Sally.[30]

Sally shared how Raun was once labeled severely autistic and mentally retarded. His parents chose to see hope for him despite the limited future and the doom and gloom predicted by the medical experts. They loved him for his uniqueness and, rather than forcing him to join their world, they joined his exclusive world. Rather than judge his plate twirling, hand flapping, endless rocking, and staring silently as inappropriate, his parents believed his actions comforted him and that he was doing the best he could with the information he had.

Both his parents, Barry (Bears) and Samarhia Kaufman, accepted Raun for who he was beyond the limits of the labels, and pioneered a therapy based on unconditional love and acceptance. Raun came out of autism at age four with no traces of his former condition and is now an amazing teacher at the Option Institute.

Gratefully I paid attention to how deeply this message of hope and acceptance resonated with me that day. When I think about it, I have moved mountains of self-limiting beliefs to get to the wonderful place I am in now. Doing the Son-Rise Program® with my children has taught me to see the Divine in each of them, in my older son, in me, in my husband, in all others. What a glorious gift this is!

One of the most effective tools I used to moving the mountains of self-limiting beliefs was the Option Process® Dialogue. I gave myself the gift of being with the best-trained mentors. I continually explored my beliefs, and the mentors provided a loving, accepting presence, listening without directing or guiding. Each mentor held the intention to help me create the answers by believing I was my own best expert. Through this self-examination process, I moved mountains of the limiting beliefs about myself and my children. I liberated myself from feeling that life as a parent of two special learners was a burden, and hard. I have now been living the Son-Rise experience for three years.

I want to share the turning point in my awareness, which I see as the cracking open of my divine consciousness. During a visualization exercise at the parenting class at the Option Institute, the teacher guided us to visualize a happy, enjoyable moment with one of our children to capture our feelings of being with our child. I chose Marion. I visualized us playing in the Son Rise room I had constructed at home. I am blowing bubbles and watching her excitement and delight in tracking each bubble as it floated in the air and then spontaneously popping. Then I visualized rocking on the floor on my back with Marion balanced on my feet getting a ride. I was instructed to capture the feelings we have never expressed verbally to our child. Joy came to my mind, the feeling of joy at playing with Marion.

I couldn't wait to arrive at home from yet another amazing week at the Option Institute. That night, putting Marion to bed, I shared my feelings with her, "Marion, you bring me such joy." She momentarily held eye contact, a rare event at that time. She was amazingly still and present while looking at me, then she rubbed my back and said "**joy**." That was the turning point. I saw Marion in that instant as the wise, spiritual soul she truly is and I saw through the veil of the label of Down syndrome. I saw the divine soul that is Marion. That event was the beginning of my understanding that we are all connected and we are all divine if we choose to see. How grateful I am to Marion for giving me the opportunity to see and create that experience for myself!

The Three Stories

As with most parents of children with labels, the three mothers in these stories went through a period of profound pain and suffering in relation to parenting their children. At some point, they realized there had to be a better way to exist than the constant pain and worrying. There was a glimmer of an idea that perhaps they could have peace instead of the suffering. Each one approached the task differently, however, each one eventually found relief by going inward and examining the beliefs each held about parenting, about his/her life, and who each is. Each one began to realize she was in a spiritual classroom, although each used different words to describe this.

This going inward means taking the time to listen, to open up to a new way of being. There is nothing fun about beginning to examine the dark thoughts. It requires trust in the process and an unshakable desire to find peace. As my son Tyler so aptly wrote, "It's good to be bitter and broken sometimes because that's when the most powerful emotions are expressed. And those lead you to hope, when all light is dim."

I would add that hope is a positive emotion that begins the process of being able to create a more positive life story. Eventually this process will help you realize that you do not need hope to access the peace within. Katie is learning to accept with gratitude the life she was given, instead of mourning for a life that will never be. Deirdre learned that she lives in grace and is the creator of her own story of infinite possibilities. Mary Pat's divine consciousness was cracked open when she saw the divine light in her daughter. Each one is offered opportunities over and over again to see their children with fresh eyes, *as if for the first time*.

For each mother in these stories, the inquiry process continues, as it does for all of us. We create a more positive story for ourselves, however, the ego will always sabotage our efforts, and so the process of inquiry is continual. We constantly need to look at the dark thoughts and bring them to light. And we know we need to do this every time we judge someone for their beliefs, every time we get angry with our partner or spouse, every time we are disgusted with a politician, every time we feel despair over our children's struggles.

Creating a more positive story brings us one step closer to accepting what is and the realization that we do not need any story to be at peace. We can always change our story by changing our thoughts about an event. And our thoughts change by uncovering self-limiting beliefs, which then allows us to just observe. Remember, beliefs are thoughts with emotions attached. We cannot force different thoughts, we can only meet them gently, understanding they are just thoughts, just observing them. Eventually, we will see the insanity of beating ourselves up over our children's struggles and the thoughts will let go, to be replaced by more loving thoughts.

Loving without Fear

The next story is from Nouk Sanchez and Tomas Viera about their daughter, Rikki. Nouk and Tomas, authors of *Take Me to Truth, Undoing the Ego*, are teachers of *A Course in Miracles* and they wrote the foreword to this book. Their story of parenting their daughter through a life-threatening crisis demonstrates immense courage in releasing all judgment about their daughter's situation, trusting in the divine wisdom in their daughter, and trusting the Unified Spirit to lead the way to inner peace, no matter the outcome.

Nouk and Tomas

Our daughter was around fourteen years old when it happened. The signs of weight loss and purging became increasingly evident until I realized that history was repeating itself. Thirty-seven years ago, at the same age, I had suffered from anorexia and although I had kept this secret carefully hidden from Rikki in an effort to protect her, here now was the exact same illness resurfacing yet again. Tomas and I had a typical initial response – panic. This was followed by numerous medical consultations including visits with three separate psychologists. Yet, in spite of these professionals' best intentions, Rikki's state of health was rapidly declining.

Being long-time *A Course in Miracles* students, Tomas and I had learned by then how to access, distinguish, and trust the divine inner wisdom that each of us has. We call it the Unified Self, which is the fully aware part of our mind that is in direct communication with uninterrupted love at all times. Our guidance revealed that Rikki's crisis was not going to be healed through regular means, ie. psychology.

We were shown that her illness was a manifestation of a far more profound challenge than that of anorexia. We saw the illness was just a *symptom* of a much greater call for healing. This was an appeal for a decision that all of us will eventually undertake and make – the call to awaken to our Unified Self and its sacred purpose.

We recognized the pattern; there are no accidents. Tomas and I had fervently asked to grow spiritually and to be shown the perfect path. Slowly, we came to remember something; that every seeming 'break-down' (ie. illness) is always an attempt and therefore a chance to 'break through.' The false self (ego) never wants us to know this. It always seeks to restore itself, resisting like all hell the thought of *breaking through* our old beliefs and values. It was evident that while Rikki was labeled medically as being anorexic and bulimic, we decided eventually not to choose to believe or use those labels with her. We began to see this in a different context, appreciating it more as a *spiritual crisis* rather than a physical one. And we knew that this was going to take time to heal and that we needed to exercise our spiritual trust muscles like we never had before.

To accommodate her healing we literally had to 'go to Spirit' with every decision. It became obvious that she couldn't continue in school, which challenged us even further. For eighteen months she survived on less than four hours sleep every day; she withdrew from life, hiding in the darkness of her room. She did, however, journal daily and express her deep despair through art – most of which was self-depicted and gruesome, yet immensely cathartic.

As Rikki's state of mind deteriorated, our commitment to help her intensified. She became so depressed that she wanted to take her own life. The last psychologist appointment ended in a nightmare – a threat to me, the mother, to have Rikki admitted to the psychiatric ward by that night. I was told that she displayed all the symptoms of possible suicide and she now required intense psychiatric care, together with drugs and possible shock treatment, in the hospital. He implied that if Rikki was not admitted that night, and if she did suicide, then it would be due to great negligence on my part.

In panic, Tomas and I sat and asked for higher guidance despite the terror we felt. We knew this was life or death but we also knew our daughter well enough to know that hospitalization would, in itself, kill her spirit. She had already told us that the professionals she'd seen did not even recognize her real dilemma. On some level she knew that she was going through a medically unrecognized spiritual crisis, a *breakdown* in order to facilitate a *break-through*. They were treating her as if she needed 'fixing' instead of reinforcing and nurturing her transmutation and transformation process. Her ego was dying. Something inside her knew that, as painful as it was, it was her *false* self falling away to reveal her *eternal* self beneath it. Yet, the medical model attempted to *rescue and repair* her ego; the very 'self' that caused the suffering in the first place. She was so disheartened by their inability to recognize her true self and their failure to encourage this self beneath the false self that was dropping away. They only seemed to see and value the false, ego self – sadly blind to the sacred metamorphosis that was right before their eyes. They were unable to reassure her that all was well; that she was, indeed, whole and holy and that all that was happening was that it was time for the caterpillar to become the butterfly and set its self free.

We understood we had to mirror to her that she was whole and holy no matter what others were saying and then it came time to make the dreaded decision whether to hospitalize her – or not. It was a critical time for us all. Rikki could take her life in an instant. This we knew. Yet, we trusted our inner Teacher for guidance far more than external sources. We sat with Rikki, explaining the doctor's advice to hospitalize her. She said *"no,"* no hospital under any circumstances. Our response to Rikki was this: *"Okay, no hospital then, as we know it would kill you. So sweetheart, can you please at least promise us that you won't take your life? At least promise us that?"* She responded, *"No, I can't — I can't promise you that."* Tomas and I were desperate. We saw then, that if she had promised us what *we* wanted to hear, she'd be lying both to us and to herself and all that we truly wanted between us was deep joining, connection, and love.

What happened next was absolutely astounding. We sat in deep prayer asking what to do. We admitted we knew nothing. We had no idea what to do. Then, emptied of arrogance and filled with humility, what came out of our mouths and souls was this: *Sweetheart, we trust that deep down (your own inner Teacher) you know exactly what you need. And it doesn't matter what you decide to do, even if you choose to end your life, we want you to know that we love you now and forever — no shame and no guilt. We know that you are eternal and whole no matter what."*

What happened in that instant? We let go. We surrendered our fear that Rikki's body would die and in that instant she knew — knew without a doubt — that we loved her, unconditionally and eternally. She knew nothing would threaten our love. And we knew it too. We knew this love was unassailable even in the face of death. We *saw* her, possibly for the first time and in being *seen*, she had no more reason to be sick. Her profound recovery, without drugs or hospitalization, began at the instant we *let her go in love;* the second we put our selfish fears and guilt aside.

Today, five years later, Rikki is a healthy and vibrant young woman who is passionate in her creativity and spirituality. Interestingly, she has no regrets about that three-year period; her 'dark night of the soul.' So much was revealed and undone simultaneously for all of us. Previous to this, Tomas and I thought we were parenting Rikki, but during this *breakdown* and *breakthrough*, we came to appreciate that Rikki was indeed *our* teacher. And we are the lucky parents who have finally recognized the value of our wonderful daughter who taught us how to love and I mean really love — with *no* fear.

Spiritual Crisis versus Psychiatric Disorder

I find Nikki's story particularly compelling, especially the idea that what the medical profession calls a psychiatric crisis is actually a spiritual crisis, the slow destruction of the ego or the false sense of self. I hope that if you are a parent of a child who has been labeled with a psychiatric disorder such as severe depression, bipolar disorder or schizophrenia that you trust the Unified Spirit to be your teacher. Consider your child is going through a spiritual crisis caused by awareness at some level that their false sense of self is being destroyed. Rather than seeing your child as broken, defective, and disordered you can see them as persons and souls in struggle. As Nouk and Tomas so poignantly wrote about Nikki, your child will know that you love them unconditionally and trust their inner wisdom to find their way, then true healing can begin.

The psychiatric profession is firmly grounded in the ego, denying the truth of who we are. There are some people who have recovered from bipolar disorder and schizophrenia realizing they were experiencing a psychospiritual crisis. Peter Breggin is one of the leading psychiatrists espousing this view. There are many stories of psychiatric survivors who talk about their spiritual crisis and their healing separate from traditional hospitalization and medication. Their stories can be helpful. The National Empowerment Center is one place to start.

Mourning Our Children

In most parenting workshops and books about children with special-needs labels, time is spent on the idea that parents must mourn the loss of the child they thought they were going to get in order to appreciate the child they did get. It is a constant challenge to take what life gives us and find meaning. A well-known story by Emily Pearl Kingsley describes what it is like for parents when they discover their child has a disability. Imagine you have planned a trip to Italy. You have learned the language and the culture, and you are excited about being in Italy. But when you finally arrive and get off the plane, you realize that you have landed in Holland instead. Now you have to plan differently, learn a whole new language, get to know a whole new set of people with different customs and ways of being, and you also have to give up on your dream of being in Italy.[31] But as Kingsley writes, "if you spend your life mourning the fact that you didn't get to Italy, you may never be free to enjoy the very special, the very lovely, things about Holland."[32]

Katie knew this story but felt there was not a lot that was lovely about parenting Spencer. It took her a while to understand that letting go of the belief that she was supposed to have a different life was necessary to create the space for the lovely things about parenting Spencer to occur. Deirdre and Mary Pat went through a similar process.

Another way to lessen the grip of mourning for the child you hoped for and expected to have is to see the world through your child's eyes. The grief may feel real but it has nothing to do with the child. Too often when we label a child with a disability we follow by saying I wish my child did not have autism, Down syndrome, dyslexia, attention deficit disorder, bipolar disorder, or whatever is your child's label. What parents are actually saying is they wish their child did not exist and they had a different "normal" child. Imagine what this conveys to your child and how s/he feels.

Loving your child unconditionally means loving all parts of your child, the stuff you do not understand that makes you uncomfortable as well as the good stuff. We do not want to get sucked into the shame and blame game; however, children's behavior changes when they are accepted for who they are. This is why the Son Rise Program® can be so effective; adults join the child's world in total acceptance rather than forcing the child to join the adult's world.

People within the autism spectrum have been around long enough for the adults to now write about and express what it is like to grow up with autism and they have much wisdom to impart, which is applicable to all the different labels we give children. Jim Sinclair, an adult with autism writes, "You didn't lose a child to autism. You lost a child because the child you waited for never came into existence. That isn't the fault of the autistic child who does exist, and it shouldn't be our burden. We need and deserve families who can see us and value us for ourselves, not families whose vision of us is obscured by the ghosts of children who never lived. Grieve if you must, for your own lost dreams. But don't mourn *us*. We are alive. We are real, and we're here waiting for you."[33]

Sometimes in our spiritual journey we try so hard to release limiting beliefs that all we do is bury the belief; we often do nothing but deny our pain. Sometimes I judge myself the most harshly when I decide I have learned nothing from all my inquiry work. I have all this knowledge and I still struggle. We are here in this physical body doing the best we can, as is everyone else; pretending otherwise does not help anyone. So we do the normal stuff: go to the doctor's, consult the professionals, parent and advocate for our child.

What is different is our attitude. We mourn for the dream of the child we thought we were going to get and then move on, seeing past the label to the whole child, listening to our children without judgment, seeing the divine light in our children and in every person we meet, choosing the Unified Spirit as our teacher instead of the ego, continuing with our inquiry work, and observing our thoughts. As demonstrated in the powerful story about Nouk and Tomas's daughter, ultimately we will learn to trust, let go, and surrender to the Unified Spirit's plan for us and our children, even during those times of extreme crisis. And when we do, we start to remove the blocks to love's awareness, remembering the truth of who we are for everyone.

Chapter VIII

Summary Points

In the end, kindness is all that matters.
–Hands by Jewel

I cannot emphasize enough the importance of choosing to believe that we are in a spiritual classroom rather than an accidental life full of obstacles. I begin each day with the intent to see each event as a spiritual lesson taught by the Unified Spirit. Inner peace is only attained by wanting it above everything else. At times what I am learning feels miraculous, and a whole lot of the times it feels like an impossible task to just observe with the Unified Spirit and not judge all the people in my life.

Any time we feel any resistance in the form of fear, judgment, discomfort, uneasiness, pain, sadness, or grief, we have chosen the ego as our teacher instead of the Unified Spirit. So doing our inquiry work is continual, it never ends. However, with practice, we eventually get better at observing our thoughts without judgment. More and more we start feeling an unshakable calm within.

Sometimes when we go within to look at and question long-held beliefs, it feels worse before it gets better. Undoing the ego can be scary work because our identity, the person we believe we are, feels threatened as we examine long-held, cherished beliefs. We really do not want to see all those frightening places inside us. Ultimately we will have to answer the question of who we are without our beliefs. Also, we would rather project our unhappiness onto others so we can blame them for our suffering. And as much as we would like to blame some of our pain on our child's disability or disorder, the diagnosis or disabling condition has nothing to do with it. The Unified Spirit sees past the veil of our ugliness and shame, and sees it for what it is — nothing, for in reality, we are loving creations of God.

The following analogy may not be very appealing, however, it may express what it feels like to look at the egoic thought system and let it go. I have a touchy stomach so I easily become nauseated after I eat something that disagrees with me. It always happens at night. I will lie in bed doing yoga breathing and anything to avoid throwing up. Yet when I give in and throw up, I immediately feel better. When you give in and surrender to examining the dark thoughts with the Unified Spirit as your teacher, you will feel better. It may be initially painful but, once you do it, you will feel relief as love enters.

It took awhile but now I find it immensely comforting to know I do not have to control or fix my family and friends in order for all of us to be happy. All I need do is change my mind, my perceptions. We are taught to be problem solvers, to fix things, to change the world. It is a relief to realize that all I need do is change my mind about the world. It is never the person or event causing pain or pleasure; it is our interpretation of the person or event.

We can still do all those things that we were doing before as physical bodies, only now we see with the eyes of the Unified Spirit and we act in this world from love, seeing past the veil of darkness to the divine spirit in every person. We hold the light and wholeness of our children for others to see and in so doing, we also hold the light and wholeness for our family and friends and for all those professionals who work with our children.

I have presented lots of ideas and concepts about parenting our children, especially those with labels. Parenting is a process of going inward and looking at all those places of resistance to loving what is. Only then can we parent from a place of peace. And when we do this our children benefit and learn from our inward calm. Peace, no matter what is happening around us, comes from forgiving people by looking with non-judging eyes.

On the level of form there may be consequences to behavior, on the level of spirit we know we are innocent. This is a gradual and continual process and there are many steps that help us to remove the blocks to love's awareness. The following is a summary of those steps as discussed in this book. They are not stages or necessarily chronological. They are just suggestions to use, if helpful, on your parenting journey of forgiveness, seeing with the eyes of love without judgment, loving without fear.

- **Embrace life as if you chose it**

Embrace your life as if you chose it. We must be able to accept that we chose our lives with all its struggles and suffering. We must realize we chose the ego as our teacher and thus this is why we are here, only then will we be able to rise above it and find a way to live in peace. We cannot skip the steps of being in this life until we can look at the ego thought system and say I do not want this.

- **Choose to see all life as a spiritual classroom rather than a series of obstacles to endure or overcome.**

Sometimes we feel as if we are in a prison of our child's suffering and our suffering. Sometimes, it feels like "frozen grief." When we can change our perception to embrace each event as a spiritual lesson, then the grief begins to thaw and we let in the voice of the Unified Self to be our teacher. We start recognizing the blessings and the process of forgiveness begins, which is the undoing of the ego's thought system of guilt, pain, and suffering. The essence of being in a spiritual classroom is to use the form, which is our belief in being a physical body, to get at the content of oneness and love. We choose the Unified Spirit as our teacher instead of the ego. We greet each day with the peaceful thought that every challenging, stressful, or painful experience is an opportunity to learn forgiveness. Each lesson speeds us on our path home to God.

• **See your children with fresh eyes as if *for the first time*.**

One of the ways to see your children with fresh eyes is to see past the label to the whole child. Seeing our children as if *for the first time* means we see our children without all the assumptions implied by the label. When we see the truth of our children, we deny giving any power to the label. On the level of spirit, we know we are all one and we forgive the labels we give ourselves and our children, the labels that perpetuate exclusion and separation from others. Sometimes seeing our children with fresh eyes means setting aside a time each day to sit in silence and hold the image of your child in the light of God's love.

• **See the world through your child's eyes.**

Seeing the world through your child's eyes means looking at the situation from their perspective. We usually try to force children into our world, our way of perceiving, without trying to understand what is going on with them. We make assumptions about behavior all the time and then act from those assumptions. More often than not the assumptions are not true to the child. This negates what the child is feeling and experiencing. When we see the world through the child's eyes, we can forge understanding and trust in our child's divine wisdom.

• **Give yourself the gift of a question.**

When we are stuck in the ego thought system of suffering, or when we are feeling any type of resistance to loving what is, it is time to ask a question. It is time to do some inquiry work, some self examination. There are no neutral thoughts, because they are always associated with judgment of past events. It is difficult to let go of egoic thoughts without first understanding the beliefs (thoughts with emotions attached) that are driving our responses to people's actions and events. Once we uncover a long-held, limiting belief, we observe and turn it over to the Unified Spirit until it is released as not being useful. We can then create a more positive story. Creating a more positive story about the events in our life can help us eventually accept whatever happens as perfect for our learning. We begin to realize we do not need our stories in order to be happy. It is a process. We now understand that each life event is a forgiveness lesson in relinquishing the ego in this spiritual classroom.

- **Embrace the idea that we are all doing the best we can with the information and awareness we have in any one moment.**

We are always doing the best we can whether we are stuck in misery and the ego or open to new possibilities through listening to the voice of the Unified Spirit. When we can accept that our children are doing the best they can, we can see their struggles as a call for love. The idea that every person is always doing the best he or she can is closely associated with the process of self examination. When we realize everyone is responding to events based on deeply held beliefs of self preservation then we can forgive them their actions. We understand they have chosen the ego for their teacher. By continuing to convey the message to our children that their struggles do not define them, and by refusing to join in their limited perceptions, we bring the darkness to light. If each one of us is always doing the best we can with the information and awareness we have, then we are all innocent.

- **Trust, let go of fear, and surrender to what is.**

Trust in the Unified Spirit's plan for us on our journey of forgiveness is the key to letting go of fear which manifests as self-limiting beliefs and judgment of others. Then we can surrender to what is. When we realize our life is unfolding perfectly in this spiritual classroom, we see the blessings in every lesson, no matter the outcome. The outcome may not be what you hoped would happen or even what you think it should be. However when you surrender to what is, then you see the perfection in the learning and you feel blessed and at peace. *A Course In Miracles* says:

> You do not walk alone. God's angels hover near and all about.
> His Love surrounds you, and of this be sure; that
> I will never leave you comfortless.[34]

• **Be kind when all else fails.**

All of us, no matter what spiritual path we have embraced, will at times feel that our path has the answers and we know best. Feeling that we are right and everyone else is wrong, is the ego's trap. If we are feeling inclined to impose our own beliefs on someone else, it is helpful to remember that we have fallen into the ego's trap of judgment. The Unified Spirit uses whatever symbols and beliefs people are following at the time to lead them to the truth. It is not up to us to judge their path. We can either be right or we can have a relationship. We can either be right or we can be at peace. If we are struggling not to judge someone else's path, actions, or opinions, then just be kind. If you do not know what else to do, if you do not know how to help your child, if you are knocked out of your calm, if you are unable to hear the voice of the Unified Spirit, then ask yourself, what is the kindest thing you can do?

Remember your spiritual path is just for you, no one else. We do not have to move mountains or have a deep spiritual experience to be kind, and release judgment. The everyday, little kindness matters. We know what is kind and what is not, just by how we feel; whether the kindness did or did not bring us peace. Being kind means realizing we all chose to be here – we are all in this together.

Sometimes we have to fake it to make it. Until recently, every time Tyler got another tattoo, I would go into judgment and fear that he was ruining his future. Tyler learned to warn me through an email that he would arrive at home with another tattoo. So I would fake an interest in his tattoos, asking about them and what they signified. (Tyler designs his own tattoos.) Eventually I became fascinated by what they mean to Tyler and how beautiful they are. I started seeing life through Tyler's eyes. I begin to drop my judgments. I remember that Tyler is on his own spiritual journey and I have no idea what his lessons are. His story is not my story. I can see him as if for the first time. And slowly I remember that each of us is doing the best we can with the information and awareness we have.

When your child is fearful, resentful, raging, unhappy, obstinate, sad, upset, acting bizarrely, or struggling in any way, and you observe yourself judging and do not know what to do, turn it over to the Unified Spirit and just be kind. Try to see the world through your child's eyes and ask yourself what would feel kind if you were your child. The act of kindness for someone else often loosens the grip of dislike and also your own suffering. On the level of form, sometimes the kindest thing we can do, no matter how small, loosens the ego's grip.

Ultimately, kindness without judgment is realizing that we do not have to fix our children because they are not broken. All we can do is change our mind and see with the eyes of love without fear. Relax into peace, God is with you always and forever.

Chapter IX

The Miracle of Forgiveness

"But I don't want to go among mad people," Alice remarked.
"Oh, you can't help that," said the Cat. "We're all mad here.
I'm mad. You're mad."
"How do you know I'm mad?" said Alice.
"You must be," said the Cat, "or you wouldn't have come
here."
–Lewis Carroll, *Alice's Adventures in Wonderland*

One of the teachings of *A Course in Miracles* that can be difficult for both students and people new to the *Course* is the metaphysical idea that this world and everything in it is an illusion and insane because it is ruled by the egoic thought system of sin, guilt, and suffering. Like Alice, we think we are not mad and do not want to be "among mad people." We prefer to believe that it is possible to find sanity and happiness and that there is much about this physical world to inspire and transform. However as Arten, one of Gary Renard's spiritual teachers says in *Disappearance of the Universe,* "Your unconscious mind, which you are completely oblivious to or else it wouldn't be unconscious, is under the domination of a sick thought system that is shared on both a collective and individual level by everyone who comes to the false universe — or else they wouldn't have come here in the first place. This will remain the case until your thoughts are examined, correctly forgiven, released to the Holy Spirit, and replaced by His thinking instead. Until then your hidden beliefs will continue to dominate and assert themselves in a predetermined way. The world is merely acting out a symbolic scenario that each one here agreed to participate in before they ever appeared to arrive."[35]

How we manage being in this illusory world caused by the insane thought of separation from God while forgiving this insanity comprises the teachings of *A Course in Miracles*. It is very often our children with labels who propel us to see the insanity of the suffering in the world, or at least to question whether there is a better way to parent and be in relationship with others. When we change our mind about the world, we can recognize the insanity of the egoic thought system and instead, with the undoing of the ego, create "happy dreams of love."[36] And because parenting is such a major relationship in our lives, it offers a perfect spiritual classroom for doing this.

By practicing the principles of *A Course in Miracles*, individuals may find their own path back to God. *A Course in Miracles* is a not a religion. Instead, it is a teaching tool to help us change our minds and remember that we are at one with God and, in fact, never left. It is a tool for helping us remove the blocks to the awareness of love's presence.[37] The *Course* emphasizes there are many paths to this truth and all of us return to God in the end. If *A Course in Miracles* does not speak to you, then the Unified Spirit or Holy Spirit, as it is called in the *Course*, will lead you to something else.

This chapter includes a description of my experience becoming a student of *A Course in Miracles* and a more in-depth interpretation and understanding of some of the teachings of *A Course in Miracles* in relation to the ideas presented in this book. I am a student, not an expert teacher. Because this is a complex teaching tool for undoing the ego, I can only understand it from the awareness I have right now. The more I study the *Course*, the deeper my understanding. So long as I see myself as a physical body, I still believe in separation and therefore there is much more I need to learn.

This chapter is for students of *A Course in Miracles* and for those who are curious to learn more about it. It is not meant to be a comprehensive explanation of its teachings. If that is what you are seeking, please refer to the resource section of this book for suggestions.

Immediate Lessons in Forgiveness

I was led to *A Course in Miracles* by reading Gary Renard's book, *Disappearance of the Universe*. The message of *A Course in Miracles* stunned me. I felt a profound truth had been revealed but it led to a period of intense questioning of my current spiritual beliefs and, for a while, I felt as if God had betrayed me. I was lost, confused, anxious, and desperate for some answers. Although it may seem counterintuitive, sticking with the study of the *Course* felt the only way out of this spiritual crisis. Choosing to become a student of *A Course in Miracles* gave six immediate lessons in forgiveness.

First, the *Course* is a channeled message from Jesus. Although I was raised as a Presbyterian, by high school I had rejected Christian teachings and thus, Jesus. Much later, as an adult, I realized I was rejecting the patriarchal organized church's inter-pretation of Jesus' teachings, and came to understand that his universal message of unconditional love is transforming. Yet, old habits and feelings die hard and I still had a difficult time separating Jesus' message from organized religion, and thus accepting Jesus as my teacher.

Second, as a feminist, I chose the spiritual path of following the Goddess in order to reintroduce the sacred feminine into patri-archal religious teachings. The masculine language of the *Course* was a turnoff and made me angry.

Third, and closely associated with using the Goddess as my symbol of the divine, is the non-dualism of *A Course in Miracles*. I always considered that God embodied both the masculine and feminine energies. The masculine energy worked in the world as God and the feminine energy worked in the world as the Goddess. So following the Goddess was my way of bringing balance to our patriarchy-dominated religions.

Fourth, I struggled to understand the concept of the one mind. I embrace the idea that Jesus is not God's only son but that instead, everyone is an offspring of God, which makes up the one sonship. What is difficult to grasp is the one mind that split between the Holy Spirit (our unified higher self) and the ego.

Fifth, the idea that God does not act in this world felt like abandonment.

And sixth, I had trouble accepting the idea that deep within our collective unconscious we are actually afraid of God for our act of defiance in believing in separation, which generates deep guilt and hatred for others.

In *A Course in Miracles*, the symbol of the Holy Spirit represents God's voice in this physical world, which is our remembrance of our higher self, at-one with God. In this book, I substituted the words Unified Spirit because I believe many of you reading this book have rejected traditional Christianity's interpretation of the Holy Spirit. The Unified Spirit or our unified higher self signifies the unity of our connection with God.

In A *Course in Miracles* the Holy Spirit can be used synonymously with Jesus. For all practical purposes they are one and the same. It has taken awhile for me to forgive Jesus for what our traditional churches have done to him and his teaching. There are many people who still have a problem with the Jesus of organized religion; therefore I did not use him as a symbol in this book. Being able to listen to the voice of Jesus can personalize A *Course in Miracles* for its students. For example, it may feel easier for some to have a personal conversation with Jesus rather than the abstract idea of the Holy Spirit. Forgiving Jesus means forgiving my projection of judgment on those who choose to follow the Christianity of organized religion. This is a huge forgiveness lesson that makes A *Course in Miracles* a perfect spiritual curriculum for me to follow.

Another profound lesson was to forgive the book's use of masculine instead of gender-neutral language. I heard of a woman who changed all of the masculine words to gender-neutral words throughout the entire A*Course in Miracles*. This is a major undertaking, as the total A *Course in Miracles* is extremely lengthy. Writing in gender-neutral language felt too time–consuming, so first I tried to change the language mentally as I read the *Course*. This rapidly became very tedious and limited my ability to focus on the message. Instead, I chose to embrace the essence of A *Course in Miracle* teachings and forgive my need for gender-neutral language.

Forgiving the masculine language was not easy because I have built much of my identity on promoting women. This involves affirming instead of devaluing those feminine attributes such as cooperation, nurturance, and service, and righting the wrongs and abuses women have experienced for a very long time. At times this led to intense anger at men in general, which was certainly not a peaceful place to be. By the time I became a student of A *Course in Miracles*, I had begun the process of releasing the anger, as I realized it was destroying my peace of mind and was not useful for healing relationships. So A *Course in Miracles* provided another step in the journey, but it was a huge one.

Letting go the belief that the men and women who embrace the values of patriarchy such as dominance and control, are responsible for all that is wrong with this world, required a lot of inquiry and self examination. While it appears minor, I knew I was successful when I could read A *Course in Miracles* and not even notice the masculine language.

It was difficult learning to understand that I am projecting onto others my own anger, not the other way around.This is where people constantly trip up, forgiving everyone on the level of spirit while still acting in this world without projecting our guilt and hatred. I think this is particularly difficult for those of us promoting social justice causes. The main criticism I hear over and over again about *A Course In Miracles* is the idea that we cannot fix this world. To people who do not understand *A Course In Miracles* teachings and many who think they do, this sounds like a message to do nothing. It feels like a cop-out and the ego is quick to get on board with the guilt.

I have struggled a lot with this, how to do what I feel called to do and reconcile it with not fixing the world. Our forgiveness lessons come from being in this world through our social interactions with family, friends, co-workers, acquaintances, and our perceptions of people we never meet but read or hear about. Totally withdrawing from the world and doing nothing can also be an act of judgment. Forgiveness comes from changing our minds about what we are doing to seeing with the eyes of love rather than the eyes of judgment. So we do what we are called to do; only we ask the Holy Spirit or Jesus to be our teacher rather than the ego. When the Holy Spirit becomes our teacher, then we extend God's love into whatever we do. Therefore it does not matter what we do, making widgets or fighting to correct the injustices we see in the world, so long as we are an extension of love's presence to everyone, including those who appear to be our enemies.

A key to understanding *A Course in Miracles* is the concept of non-dualism. Dualism is a function of this physical world; it's what fuels the ego's thought system of judgment and projection. There are men and there are women. There are "normal" children and there are children with disabilities. Hatred is needed in order to understand love. God sends us pain and suffering so we can learn to be better people. Because there is so much hatred in the world, there must be a dark side to God.

I suspect that most people reading this book would say they believe God is love and that we are God's creations. If so, then it brings up some problematic questions. If God is perfect love, then how could s/he create something as imperfect as this world? If God is love, then how come so many people suffer? For God to create flawed human beings must either mean that he is imperfect or that he deliberately created us so we could mess up, fail, suffer, and be punished by him. This is insane. How can that be a God of love?

The pure non-dualism of *A Course in Miracles* teaches that God is perfect, limitless Love and because we are extensions of God's love, we are also perfect, limitless, pure spirit. Thus none of this physical world can be real and cannot be from God. If we are perfect extensions of God's love then we have to be dreaming this mistake of separation.

While initially I felt abandoned by God as a new student of *A Course in Miracles*, eventually I realized God could not abandon something s/he did not create. I had always struggled with the seeming contradiction of believing in an all-loving God and the cruelty and violence that exist in the world. Recognizing that God does not cause this worldly mess but that we do, in this illusion, allows belief in an all-loving God.

Our reality is that we are loving extensions of God. Yet sometime in the very ancient past, we had a mistaken thought that we could be separate from God. In that instant, the ego thought-system that created this world and universe was born. Symbolically, we fell asleep and are dreaming this life of illusion. God left us with the voice of the Holy Spirit to gently awaken us from this dream of struggle, contradiction, and periodic pain. God does not act in this world because it is an illusion, and to do so would make the mistake real.

After a lengthy internal struggle, I was able to embrace as

freeing the idea that God does not intervene in this world. I could wholeheartedly embrace a loving God that exists outside time and space. I have the power within to choose to see the illusion with God's loving eyes to the perfect unity of everything.

If we are at-one with God and perfect extensions of his love, then it follows that there is only one mind. This one mind split into the Holy Spirit and the ego with the mistaken thought of separation. The Holy Spirit is our memory of our higher unified self at-one with God. Therefore there is also only one ego, which manifests as many in order to perpetuate the illusion that we are physical bodies and separate from God. This really is a difficult idea to swallow because we see things from our personal perspective, whose purpose is to keep us thinking we are individuals separate from others. We get confused between our brain and the one mind.

How can all the people in the world possibly be just one ego split into many? I can drive myself crazy trying to figure this out, which is just what the ego wants. Yet the more I practice the forgiveness of *A Course In Miracles,* the more my level of awareness increases until I catch glimpses of the perfection of it all. It just is. Everything in this dream, just is, just thoughts, nothing else.

At some point, all students of *A Course In Miracles* will ask how an all-loving God could allow the mistaken thought of separation to occur. This is a question of the ego, and there are no answers on the level of form, this physical existence. At some deep level I understand that there can be no answer to this question because it is the ego's trick or a "catch 22" to reinforce our belief in separation. And when I am angry at another person, I understand I am actually angry with God for allowing us to stray. I think this idea of deep, unconscious guilt, hatred, and fear of God's wrath often manifests as intense anger at God. It drives the ego, and thus our belief in physical bodies. This ancient, unconscious, hatred and fear of God is overlooked by many students of *A Course In Miracles* and I suspect it stops other spiritual seekers from accepting *A Course In Miracles*.

I certainly believe I feel God's love and do not fear him. Yet I am beginning to have an awareness of my deeply buried fear every time I judge another. And if I am truly honest with myself, this fear often manifests as my hatred for those who perpetuate the social condition of patriarchy, which I now realize is just another symbol for the ego. And the dominance and control values of patriarchy are often what perpetuate the medical model, or deficit model, of treating our labeled children.

Thus, I try to fight patriarchy, a symbol of the ego, with the thought system of the ego. This is crazy; it is a never ending trap to project onto others my anger and guilt. So instead of mouthing the words that God is love, I need to acknowledge my hatred and fear of God and bring it to the light of God's forgiveness. Our "dark nights of the soul" give us the opportunity to bring our darkness to light. And it is often our struggling children who force us into despair and to say, "There has to be a better way?" Once we ask the question, we have started our forgiveness path to healing our guilt and anger.

The Spiritual Classroom as a Dream

We believe we are physical beings separate from other physical beings. And we perpetuate this separateness by categorizing and labeling people. We separate by gender, race, economic status, education, looks, age, intelligence, and by disability, among others factors. We can talk about oneness with people, but it is a difficult concept to actually practice. One way to practice is to remind ourselves that people are either calling for love or acting from love.[38] This means we either respond from a place of fear or we respond from the truth of who we are, which is love, peace, and joy.

Our children are doing the same thing; they are no different from us. It helps as parents to remember that when our children struggle, they are acting from fear, and calling for love. We are immortal spirits and thus our bodies are just images and have nothing to do with who we truly are. I have some understanding of these truths, yet I clearly still see myself as an individual, separate from everyone else. So I need the spiritual tools and symbols the Unified Spirit provides for my awakening journey. This is the essence of being in a spiritual classroom — to realize that each life event is a lesson in accepting that we are part of a living process of forgiveness to undo the ego and its thoughts of separation.

A Course In Miracles provides the tools to undo the ego thought system of separation, guilt and attack through the miracle of forgiveness. Forgiveness is seeing with nonjudgmental eyes. Forgiveness is realizing there is nothing anyone can do to me nor is there anything I can do to anyone else because none of this is real, it is all a part of my dream. For example, we know that the people we create in our night-time dreams represent parts of our psyche. We do not blame the people who show up in our night-time dreams for the wrongs they commit, because we know our night dreams are not real. The same principle works in our everyday lives. When we do not judge a person who has injured us, then we demonstrate that the person and we are not bodies. We forgive them for what they have not done.

We mistakenly believe that in order to regain God's love we must prove we are innocent of this thought of separation. Therefore we project onto others our fears and our guilt in order to show God we are innocent and that it is the other person's fault. It is hard to accept that we do this with our children because we would like to think we love our children uncondi-tionally. Whenever we become upset by their behavior, disability, disease, or disorder, we are projecting our guilt and saying it is not our fault. Learning to accept that I project onto my children, my spouse, and my friends, my own insecurities, has been a long process and one that is still ongoing. Not accepting our own insecurities and judgment means we blame others for what is going wrong in our life. Blaming others means we do not have to look at ourselves. It feels easier than taking the scary path of examination, which brings our dark, ugly thoughts to the light of forgiveness.

I had an "ah ha" moment recently in regard to my relationship with money. Like a good spiritual seeker, I realize on some level that it is my thoughts of scarcity based on non-existent past events that keep me fearful of not having enough. So I try to just observe these negative thoughts and then let them go — not very successfully at times. Because my understanding is tenuous, not much has to happen for the fear thoughts to return. Therefore I want my husband to do for me what I cannot do for myself and I often blame his fear thoughts about money for dragging me down. I start thinking that this is hard enough without my husband contributing to my fears. It was as if a switch went off in my head and I finally understood completely that I was blaming my husband for my fears, that I was projecting my insecurities onto him. And in so doing, I did not have to accept responsibility for my negative thoughts; he was to blame.

I finally understood, this is my hologram or dream and I made everyone up. Everyone is a part of me, yet they take on different roles or different aspects of my fears and judgments, including my children. Everyone in my dream is acting out my insecurities. My daughter, Sarah, judges herself for being unable to release sad, stressful thoughts. I have projected onto her my difficulties in doing the same. It is why sometimes, I feel inadequate to help her, because it is my inadequacy not hers. Wow, this means I can forgive them for what they have not done. It means they are innocent.

It does not help to start asking the ego questions about the interconnection between everyone else's dream or hologram or how we can be a projection in another person's dream. That will make you crazy which, is exactly where the ego wants you. However, on a higher level, it makes sense if we are all part of the one ego manifesting as many. Remember, this is a process, so if the dream or hologram idea does not resonate with you, then something else will, and when you are ready it will make sense.

On the level of spirit there is no order to the hierarchical events in this illusion, our hologram. On the level of form, this physical world, the ego convinces us that some life events are more painful than others, such as our child's disability, disease, or disorder. When we start small and learn to not judge the minor annoying events, then we can eventually apply our learning to the seemingly larger, more painful events. The miracle is to see all of this through the eyes of forgiveness, recognizing that everyone is innocent. It is a living organic process to see with the eyes of the Unified Spirit and forgive what we believe we and others have done.

God Makes No Mistakes
Originally when I was writing the chapter on "No Child is a Mistake," I titled it "God makes no mistakes." I changed it to "No Child is a Mistake" because I wanted this book to be accessible to people on all spiritual paths. The idea that there are no mistakes because God did not create this world, was a metaphysical concept I felt could more easily be discussed in this chapter on *A Course in Miracles* teachings. Therefore the following discussion will focus on the idea, "God makes no mistakes."

Many of us on our quest for spiritual enlightenment come to the awareness that we are spiritual beings having a physical experience. When we believe this, then yes, we can say "God makes no mistakes," or, "no child is a mistake," because we are perfect spiritual beings. This explanation did not quite do it for me. I believed that I was a spiritual being but I could not understand why we had to go through so much suffering while in physical form. I spent lots of time asking anguished questions about how God could be unconditional love and allow the suffering in this world. I did not care for the argument that God makes us go through pain and struggle to teach us lessons in love. As discussed in chapter five, "The Holy Encounter," this is an argument often used by people to explain the presence of children with labels in their lives. This did not feel like a loving God to me. It was only after becoming a *Course* student that I felt comfortable with the belief, "God makes no mistakes," because he did not create the world.

Once again, it is the process of using the form (our belief in a separate physical body), to get at the spiritual content of oneness and love. Our relationships are always conditional; it is how the egoic thought system of separation works. We decide a person has to be a certain way for us to be happy. Once we recognize this is true for all our relationships, including the ones we have with our children, we can begin the process of undoing the ego's need to project onto others our emotions and fears. We can begin to examine our beliefs in order to parent from a place of unconditional regard for all our children.

This is particularly compelling for parenting our labeled children. If I am dreaming, then my children are dreaming. We are in each other's dreams and agreed to this scenario before we arrived. That is all we need know; to ask why, just keeps us guessing and making no progress with answers. Thus we can see our children's situation as an opportunity for forgiveness, or we can stay stuck in the pain of how come, why me, why my child?

Once we decide our child's reality is the label, and the struggles it implies, then we have chosen the ego as our teacher. So we hold the vision of spiritual oneness for ourselves, our children, and others. We constantly return to the Unified Spirit as our teacher and convey to our children that no matter what happens in this physical life, they are, in reality, extensions of God's love. And I can do this by acknowledging that my child is in my dream, and I project onto them my guilt and suffering. Of course, I have to be vigilant in my awareness because the ego will then try hard to convince me that the dream is real and my projection onto my children is my fault. This results in turning the judgment inward and then the ego has me in its grip once again. Therefore, I remind myself that this is my dream; it is not real, therefore I am innocent, just as my children are innocent. I choose forgiveness instead of judgment.

Some labels in this dream appear to be more positive, such as the "indigo" or "crystal" child labels. However, in this physical world, these labels can be seen as just more labels with expectations of behavior. It is helpful to remind ourselves that these children's psychic gifts or extra-sensory abilities occur within this dream and therefore can be used by the ego to perpetuate the mistake of separation. On the level of spirit, we are all one. None of the labels we give ourselves or our children are real, they do not define who we are. The only truth is that we are extensions of God's love.

On the level of form, we may use the "indigo" and "crystal" labels in our spiritual classroom to honor the divine spirit within and help our children hold onto this spiritual awareness of their truth. However, it is important to remember that even if some children have a clearer remembrance of their spiritual connections, they still are born with the ego thought system intact or otherwise they would not be here in a physical body. On the level of spirit, we know we are all one and we forgive the labels we give ourselves that perpetuate the illusion of separation.

If we accept the dream as a hologram and thus that we are all connected by thought, then some people intuitively understand this idea and therefore can access abilities which we call psychic or extrasensory. These psychic or extrasensory abilities appear to us on the level of form to be spiritual because they cannot be explained by the scientific method which is the egoic thought system. After all, the ego wants us to continue to believe in this dream and is very clever about ensuring this happens. If we want to believe some of the stuff that goes on in this dream is spiritual, then the ego is happy to keep us spinning our wheels so we do not realize the truth of who we are.

A *Course in Miracles* begins by saying:

Nothing real can be threatened.
Nothing unreal exists.
Herein lies the peace of God.[39]

Reality is that we are extensions of God's love. We are eternal and cannot be threatened or destroyed. This is the world of knowledge. The world of perception is this world of birth and death, which is built on scarcity, loss, pain, and separation and therefore cannot be real because God's creations are eternal and pure love. Therefore this world is unreal, like a dream. Everything in this dream does not exist, including those things we do and do not consider to be spiritual, such as reincarnation, psychic and extrasensory abilities, organized religion, traditional medicine and alternative healing methods, the laws of attraction, and "indigo" and "crystal" children.

Once we turn over our journey to the Unified Spirit which is God's voice in this illusory world, then these things we call spiritual become a bridge to understanding and then forgiving the world. We begin to remove the blocks to love's awareness by seeing our children and others without the eyes of judgment. As I said, the ego is really clever about using what we think is our spiritual journey, or purpose, to convince us that we are on a spiritual path to enlightenment. The Unified Spirit, which speaks to us in stillness, is often filtered by the ego's voice.

As a physical being, it feels really hard to embrace the idea that there is nothing spiritual in this world because it is a mistaken dream of separation. It feels contradictory to the idea of seeing past the labels to the divinely perfect being within, or seeing God in the delicate orchid, or in the bright plumage of the macaws, or in the majesty of a mountain or in a child's smile. I have struggled with this idea and at some level I realize trying to explain it is the ego's trap to keep me believing in separation. It gets us back to the question of how any of the extraordinarily beautiful parts of earth could be a mistake? It is all about changing our minds and seeing past the illusion to the truth of who we are. Just because we are acting a part in this dream does not mean we cannot appreciate what is beautiful and inspired by our belief in God. We can use the beauty that surrounds us to see the divine in every person we encounter. "God is in everything I see because God is in my mind."[40] Deep in our soul we know that separation from God is a mistake; therefore none of this can be real because God makes no mistakes.

Forgiveness

Ken Wapnick, a teacher of *A Course in Miracles,* talks about rising above the fray and just observing the battleground of our life. It is from this detached place that we can forgive what is happening. We can be an observer of our thoughts. When we notice how our thinking shapes our feelings about an event, we begin to realize we are making it all up, even our child's disability, disease, or disorder. We can change our thinking; we can change our response to life's challenges to one of forgiveness.

It is like watching a play in which we are the actors. I am acting in my life's drama at the same time I am the director in the audience sitting next to Jesus watching my play. I do not blame or judge the people in my play because I realize they are merely acting an assigned part that I gave them. Therefore I forgive them for what they have not actually done. Sometimes all I can do is sit in the audience and observe, recognizing I still believe that the drama or the dream is true.

What I have done is project my own darkness onto you so that the light of Christ in you is obscured. By making the decision to say you are not in darkness — you are really in light, which is the decision to let go of the darkness that I have placed on you — I am really making the very same statement about myself. I am saying that not only does the light of Christ shine in you but it also shines in me. And, in fact, it is the same light. That is what forgiveness is.

Ken Wapnick, *A Talk Given on A Course in Miracles, An Introduction*[41]

What this means is that our path home to God lies with forgiving our relationships. Therefore we can be grateful for every single person in our lives, especially those who push our buttons, or who cause us the most pain, such as our children with labels.

Our path of forgiveness lies with understanding that every relationship is a special relationship because in relationship, we reenact our belief that we are separate from God. We look to relationships to fulfill our yearning for the unconditional love of God, which we think we have lost. Yet no physical being will ever be able to substitute for God's love and so they will fail us over and over again. The ego will make sure we constantly replay our disappointment by projecting our fear and guilt outside of us. So long as we follow the ego thought system, we will continue to believe that we are right and you are wrong — that the problem lies with our partners, our children, our friends, our enemies, the President, the Republicans or the Democrats, and the economic situation.

Everything perceived outside of us is actually a reflection of our inward condition. The answer to the problem of separation is within us, with the voice of the Unified Spirit. The ego does not want us to realize this because when we do, the ego disappears and we wake from this dream. Forgiveness reminds us that we already have all we need, that we are perfect, loving, eternal creations of God.

A Course in Miracles teaches that there are no neutral thoughts, because a thought always comes out of judging a past experience.[42] We see only the past.[43] Our thoughts also occur within this illusory world, so they are not real. I find I cannot begin to understand this teaching until I recognize that this whole dream is the result of a thought of separation by the one mind, until I realize my thoughts are creating my life experience. "I am responsible for what I see. I choose the feelings I experience, and I decide upon the goal I would achieve. And everything that seems to happen to me I ask for, and receive as I have asked." [44] And the way to do this for me is initially to see all events as neutral until we attach an emotion to the thoughts and then they become a belief. This is why inquiry work helps in creating a "happy dream." We uncover the beliefs that are creating our life's experience. Eventually this led to my moment of clarity when I realized I was projecting all my insecurities about money onto my husband so I did not have to own them. I am responsible for everything in my dream.

Healing

Many people who follow the teachings in new thought spirituality have a bias like me toward alternative healing methods. At the same time, I also understand there is no right, wrong, good, or bad approaches to healing; only thoughts with feelings attached, which create beliefs about what we should do. On the level of spirit, it does not matter what healing approach we use, all that matters is realizing none of this is real and we are in reality, perfect creations of God.

Therefore on the level of form, we ask the Unified Spirit to guide us toward healing methods that will assist in our forgiveness journey. The journey is toward loving what is. When we become attached to creating a story around the disability, disease, or disorder, then we fall victim to the ego, which wants us to agonize and question what to do, which healing approach to use.

The reason I have a bias toward alternative healing methods is because they appear on the level of form, to be a bridge toward understanding that actual healing occurs when we realize all of this is a dream and we are perfect creations of God. The medical model of treatment is firmly grounded in the ego and the belief that we are broken and need to be fixed. Many of the alternative healing approaches are based on the idea that we are whole and just need to find a way to get back to wholeness.

Once again, I want to emphasize that there are no right or wrong approaches, just opportunities to learn forgiveness for believing we and our children are physical bodies that can get sick, be disabled, or disordered in this spiritual classroom. On the level of spirit, we know we cannot heal these physical bodies because they are not real. Healing only occurs at the level of the one mind, forgiving our thoughts of separation. While we believe we are physical bodies, this concept of healing at the level of mind is difficult to comprehend because healing at the level of the unified mind does not necessarily translate into healing the physical body. Eventually, on this path of forgiveness, we create a happy dream in which we realize that whatever is going on with our physical bodies is of no importance, and then we are closer to waking from this dream and returning home. Until we have reached that point on our journey, any sickness, disability, or disorder is an opportunity for learning forgiveness.

Patience

Whether it is worry over our child, other people in our lives, or money, being patient with the process is the key. *A Course in Miracles* says, "Now you must learn that only infinite patience produces immediate effects."[45]

We need to be kind with ourselves and as Karen Drucker sings, "I will only go as fast as the slowest part of me feels safe to go."[46] Patience involves choosing the Unified Spirit as your teacher over the ego, over and over again. And it feels like a paradox, but when we surrender to patience, to waiting, then the results are immediate.

It is too much for us to totally comprehend all at once that we are dreaming this physical world. How could it be possible when I feel so solid, when I can look at myself in the mirror, when the vast majority of people feel all of this is real? We like our specialness and individuality that keeps us believing that our dream is real, but with it comes suffering. God left us with the voice of the Unified Spirit, our unified higher self to gently wake us to realizing that we no longer need to be an individual self with all the suffering. When we realize in the holy instant there is no dream, God brings us home to where we never left, extensions of his/her love.

I have noticed that students of *A Course in Miracles*, including myself, can get so intellectually wrapped up in the teachings that we prevent ourselves from experiencing what the *Course* is trying to convey. Seeing past the veil of darkness to the divine light within every one of us is an experience, not an intellectual exercise. Often we use lots of words to explain the metaphysics of *A Course in Miracles* yet words are just symbols used to try and explain an experience. If reading the *Course* becomes an intellectual exercise, then you know you have chosen the ego for your teacher. Moving past the words to experience the forgiveness described by Jesus maybe much more simple than we make it.

Maybe we are like Alice and have tumbled down a rabbit hole or are seeing our life as if through a looking glass. It is all topsy turvy and reflects back at us as crazy. Nothing makes sense and the more we try to figure things out by asking questions as Alice did, the crazier it gets. We are often like the Queen of Hearts, we know we are right and we want to chop off the head of everyone who disagrees with us. As the cat says, "We're all mad here." And all Alice had to do to end the craziness was wake up from her dream.

Maybe it's as simple as my singer/songwriter friend Cheryl Hoenemeyer sings in her song, "Give a Little More."

I'm getting tired of this chip on your shoulder
Doesn't make you look pretty, in fact it makes you look older
Kind of makes you look tired, kind of makes you look mean
Are you really as close to the edge as you seem
You blame the job, you blame the boss, you blame the traffic
You blame the news, the sports, the weather—yeah, it's all so automatic
You've got a list of excuses from here to LA
And I have heard them so often I know just what you'll say

And you've got to get off of this Poor Me Express
Going backwards, not forwards, or nowhere at best
And if you want a little more out of life
Give a little more of yourself[47]

As parents of children with labels, we can get caught easily in the "Poor Me Express." Maybe it is as simple as changing our minds to stop blaming everyone including ourselves. Maybe giving a little more of yourself means seeing with the eyes of love and realizing everyone is doing the best they can.

I am safe and loved, you are safe and loved, and our children are safe and loved. Perhaps all we need do is convey to our children that they are seen, heard, and whole, that they are loved for who they are. Even in this insane dream, we can change our minds to embrace everyone, including ourselves, as complete and whole offsprings of God.

Ken Wapnick, a *Course in Miracles* teacher, tells his students to go ask normal people what they do when they're in crisis. This always makes me laugh. We can get so wrapped up in trying to convince ourselves that nothing is real, we often do nothing but deny our pain. So long as we go to bed each night and wake up in a physical body, we believe in separation from God and therefore believing the dream to be true. Pretending otherwise does not help anyone. So, on the level of form, we advocate for our child in the education system, talk to their teachers, go to the doctors, and consult the professionals. What is different is our attitude. We mourn for the dream of the child we thought we were going to get and then we move on, seeing past the label to the whole child, listening to our children's stories without judgment, seeing the divine light in our children and every person we meet, choosing the Unified Spirit as our teacher instead of the ego, continuing with our inquiry work and observing our thoughts. Ultimately we will be shown, as in Nouk and Tomas's story, how to trust, let go of fear, and surrender to the Unified Spirit's plan for us and our children in this dream. And when we do, we start to remove the blocks to love's awareness and remembering the truth of who we are for everyone.

Appendix

Directions for writing a poem about your child

Write a poem and title it "Give me the spirit of my child ... (Your child's name)."

Use the following questions to write your poem.
You can start each thought with the phrase:

Please give me an impression of the spirit of (your child's name) ....

or

Please give me a sense of (child's name's) .... Spirit.

Take a moment to visualize your child each time you ask the question.

What color is your child's spirit?

If your child's spirit had a shape, what would it be?

What animal(s) best represent your child's spirit?

What part(s) of the body does your child's spirit express itself?

Where do you feel your child's spirit inside of you?

If your child's spirit had a place in the external world, where would it be?

If your child's spirit had a message, what would it be?

Resources

Spiritual books about children with labels and/or parenting:

Armstrong, Thomas *The Radiant Child* (Theosophical, Wheaton, IL, 1988)

Beck, Martha *Expecting Adam, A True Story of Birth, Rebirth, and Everyday Magic* (Berkley Books, New York, 1999)

Greene, Ross *Lost in School* (Scribner, NY,NY, 2009)
Child psychiatrist Dr Ross Greene uses a method called Collaborative Problem Solving with children labeled with behavioral problems, which provides a way to see the world through the child's eyes, to understand their perspective and then collaboratively work toward solutions that are mutually satisfactory. At his website www.livesinthebalance.org Dr Greene provides free resources and videos to take you through the process.

Greenspan, Miriam *Healing Through the Dark Emotions* (Shambhala, Boston, MA, 2004)

Kaufman, Barry Neil *Son Rise The Miracle Continues* (H J Kramer Inc., Tiburon, CA, 1994)

Martin, William *The Parent's Tao Te Ching* (Da Capo Press Lifelong Books, Philadelphia, PA, 1999)

McClure, Vimala *The Tao of Motherhood* (New World Library, Novato, CA, 1997)

Pransky, Jack *Parenting from the Heart* (Northeast Health Realization Institute, Cabot, VT, 2001)

Spangler, David *Parent as Mystic, Mystic as Parent* (Riverhead Books, New York, 1998)

Stillman, William *Autism and the God Connection, Redefining the Autistic Experience Through Extraordinary Accounts of Spiritual Giftedness* (Sourcebooks, Naperville, IL, 2006)

Stillman, William *The Soul of Autism: Looking Beyond Labels to Unveil Spiritual Secrets of the Heart Savants* (New Page Books, Franklin Lakes, NJ)

Wapnick, Kenneth *Parents and Children - Our Most Difficult Classroom, Part One and Two* (Foundation for A Course in Miracles, Temecula, CA, 2007)

Books and websites to help with inquiry and self-examination, mentioned in this book:

Katie, Byron with Stephen Mitchell *Loving What Is, Four Questions that Can Change Your Life* (Harmony Books, New York, 2002) www.thework.com

Katie, Byron with Stephen Mitchell *A Thousand Names for Joy, Living in Harmony with the Way Things Are* (Harmony Books, New York) 2007) www.thework.com

Kaufman, Barry Neil *Happiness is a Choice* (Fawcet Columbine, New York, 1994) www.option.org

Kaufman, Barry Neil *Power Dialogues the Ultimate System for Personal Change* (Epic Century Publications, Sheffield, MA, 2001) www.option.org

Books and websites about or inspired by *A Course in Miracles*

A Course in Miracles (The Foundation for Inner Peace)
The authorized three-in-one volume of *A Course in Miracles* is comprised of the Text, Workbook, and Manual for Teachers. It is available from the Foundation for Inner Peace, the original publishers. www.acim.org takes you directly to the *Course in Miracles* while www.facim.org takes you to other books and resources provided by the Foundation for Inner Peace.

Casarjian, Robin *Forgiveness, A Bold Choice for a Peaceful Heart* (Bantam Books, New York, 1992)

Jampolsky, Gerald G. *Love is Letting Go of Fear* (Celestial Arts, Berkeley, CA, 1979)
This is a wonderful book for people who are interested in learning about the main principles of *A Course in Miracles* in a practical way, without needing to understand the metaphysics.

Renard, Gary R. *The Disappearance of the Universe* (Hay House, Carlsbad, CA, 2004)
This book introduced me to *A Course in Miracles*. It concerns the illusion of our world and separation from spirit. It makes the teachings accessible and made it easier for me to read *A Course in Miracles* with greater understanding. www.garyrenard.com

Sanchez, Nouk, and Tomas Viera *Take Me to Truth, Undoing the Ego* (O Books, Winchester, U, 2007)
This book helped further my understanding of the stages we go through to undo the blocks presented by our ego. www.takemetotruth.com

The following books by Kenneth Wapnick have helped with my continuing learning and understanding of the teachings of *A Course in Miracles*:

Wapnick, Kenneth *A Talk Given on A Course in Miracles, An Introduction* (Foundation for A Course in Miracles, seventh edition, Temecula, CA, 1999).
An excellent introduction to *A Course in Miracles*.

Wapnick, Kenneth *A Vast Illusion, Time According to A Course in Miracles* (Foundation for A Course in Miracles, Temecula, CA, 2006)
A good book for explanation of the metaphysics of *A Course in Miracles*.

Wapnick, Kenneth *Ending Our Resistance to Love* (Foundation for A Course in Miracles, Temecula, CA: 2004

Wapnick, Kenneth *The Healing Power of Kindness, Volumes One and Two* (Foundation for A Course in Miracles, Temecula,CA, 2005)

All Kenneth Wapnick's books can be found at www.facim.org.

End Notes

1   *ACIM*, W-pI lesson 34

2   Gayle and Hugh Prather, *Spiritual Parenting*. (NY: Three Rivers Press, 1997) p. 31.

3   Gerald G. Jampolsky, *Love is Letting Go of Fear*. (Berkeley, CA: Celestial Arts, 1979) p. 112.

4   *ACIM*, W-pI lesson 34

5   Ursula K. Le Guin, *The Telling*. (New York: Ace Books, 2000), p. 67-68.

6   Sara Moores Campbell, *Singing the Living Tradition*. (Boston: Unitarian Universalist Association, 1993) p. 664.

7   Jack Pearpoint and Judith Snow, *From Behind the Piano: The Building of Judith Snow's Unique Circle of Friends and What's Really Worth Doing and How to Do It: A Book for People Who Love Someone labeled Disabled (Possibly Yourself)* (Toronto, Canada: Inclusion Press, 1998), p. 3.

8   Thomas Armstrong, *The Radiant Child* (Wheaton, IL: Theosophical, 1985), p. 151.

9   Thomas Armstrong, *The Myth of the ADD Child: 50 Ways to Improve Your Child's Behavior and Attention Span without Drugs, Labels, or Coercion* .(New York: Plume, 1997), p. 256.

10   Karen Drucker, "Loving Kindness" *Songs of Spirit I,* www.karendrucker.com

[11]   *ACIM*, T-in 1:6-7

[12]   The Option Institute, www.option.org

[13]   Byron Katie, *The Work*, www.thework.com.

[14]   Carol Tavris and Elliot Aronson, *Mistakes Were Made (But Not by Me) Why We Justify Foolish Beliefs, Bad Decisions, and Hurtful Acts* (New York: Harcourt, Inc., 2007)

[15]   *ACIM*, T-14.X.7:1

[16]   Karen Drucker, "Gentle with Myself" *Songs of Spirit III*, www.karendrucker.com

[17]   *ACIM*, T-14.X.7:1

[18]   L, Tobin, *What Do You Do with a Child Like This? Inside the Lives of Troubled Children* (Duluth, MN: Whole Person Associates, 1998) p. 5

[19]   L, Tobin, *What Do You Do with a Child Like This? Inside the Lives of Troubled Children* (Duluth, MN: Whole Person Associates, 1998) p. 4

[20]   *ACIM*, W-pII.289

[21]   WM. Paul Young, *The Shack* (Newbury Park, CA: Windblown Media, 2007) p. 186

[22]   Karen White, *Pieces of the Heart* (New York: New American Library, 2006) p. 166

[23]   *ACIM*, W-pI.75

24 Gerald Jampolsky and Diane V. Cirincione, *Heal Your Mind, Heal Your World,* in *The Holy Encounter* (Anaheim, CA: Miracle Distribution Center, Sep/Oct 2006) p.4

25 Karen White, *Pieces of the Heart* (New York: New American Library, 2006) p. 166

26 *ACIM,* W-pI.31

27 *ACIM,* W-pI.72

28 Kenneth Wapnick, *Memory: "The Dark Backward and Abysm of Time"* in *The Lighthouse* (Temecula, CA: Newsletter of the Foundation for *A Course in Miracles,* Vol. 20 #2 June 2009) p.3

29 David Sipress, (Boston Globe: Cartoon Parade, Parade.com/cartoons, 08/16/09)

30 Kaufman, Barry Neil. *Son Rise The Miracle Continues* (Tiburon, CA: H J Kramer Inc., 1994.)

31 Sally Patton, *Welcoming Children with Special Needs: A Guidebook for Faith Communities* (Boston: Unitarian Universalist Association, 2004) p. 20.

32 Emily Pearl Kingsley, "Welcome to Holland," www.geocities.com/Heartland/Ridge/9672/holland.html

33 Jim Sinclair, *Don't Mourn for Us* (Syracuse, NY: Autism Network International Newsletter, *Our Voice,* Vol. 1 #3, 1993)

34 *ACIM,* W-ep.6:6-8

35   Gary R. Renard, *The Disappearance of the Universe* (Carlsbad, CA: Hay House, Inc., 2004) p.16

36   *ACIM*, T-13.VII.9

37   *ACIM*, T-in.1:6-7

38   *ACIM*, T-14.X.7:1

39   *ACIM*, T-in.2:2-3

40   *ACIM*, W-pI.30

41   Kenneth Wapnick, *A Talk Given on A Course in Miracles, An Introduction* (Temecula, CA: Foundation for *A Course in Miracles*, Seventh Edition, 2006) p. 75

42   *ACIM*, W-pI.16

43   *ACIM*, W-pI.7

44   *ACIM*, T-21.II.2:3-5

45   *ACIM*, T-5.VI.9:3

46   Karen Drucker, "Gentle with Myself" *Songs of Spirit III*, www.karendrucker.com

47   Cheryl Hoenemeyer, "Give a Little More" *Crowded Bed*, www.cherylhoenemeyer@artistdirect.com

Acknowledgements

This was one of those books I knew I was supposed to write long before I actually started typing words into the computer. As I began writing, the Unified Spirit sent me constant spiritual insights about what to put into the book. They would pop into my consciousness as I went about my daily activities, so I was constantly grabbing scraps of paper to write down ideas lest I forget. Sometimes I thought I would never find organization in all the many messages and ideas swirling in my head and on scraps of paper. Whenever I got stuck or lost there was always a friend who would say the right words to bring me back to center and hearing the voice within. A special thank you to Carolyn Jensen for continually suggesting I was supposed to write this book before all the other things I thought I was supposed to do.

I would like to especially thank Katie, Mary Pat and Deirdre for contributing their inspirational stories about parenting their children and for being pioneers with me in exploring what it means to parent from a spiritual place of peace. I would also like to thank Nouk Sanchez and Tomas Viera for their teaching of *A Course in Miracles* in ways that opened new pathways of under-standing, for their unwavering support that this book was supposed to be written, for contributing their powerful story about their daughter Nikki, and writing the foreword. When I was stuck and convinced the book needed to wait till I accomplished another major activity, Nouk's guidance was invaluable in helping me open up to the Unified Spirit's voice and begin writing.

My son Tyler taught me no one is broken. He has been and still is an important teacher in this spiritual classroom called parenting. However his teaching was intertwined with and affected by the other teachers in the family, my husband Rick and my daughter Sarah as well as myself. Together we teach and we learn. This book is my thank you and tribute to them.

For More Information

Sally Patton offers workshops and presentations for parents as well as individual counseling. Please contact me if you would like to host a workshop or inquire about individual consultation.

For more information about parenting workshops individual counseling and other resources please go to my web site

www.embracechildspirit.org

BOOKS

O is a symbol of the world, of oneness and unity. In different cultures it also means the "eye," symbolizing knowledge and insight. We aim to publish books that are accessible, constructive and that challenge accepted opinion, both that of academia and the "moral majority."

Our books are available in all good English language bookstores worldwide. If you don't see the book on the shelves ask the bookstore to order it for you, quoting the ISBN number and title. Alternatively you can order online (all major online retail sites carry our titles) or contact the distributor in the relevant country, listed on the copyright page.

See our website **www.o-books.net** for a full list of over 500 titles, growing by 100 a year.

And tune in to myspiritradio.com for our book review radio show, hosted by June-Elleni Laine, where you can listen to the authors discussing their books.

mySpiritRadio